The
Nuclear Platypus
Biscuit Bible

THIS PAGE INTENTIONALLY LEFT BLANK.

(CONTRARY TO WHAT IT RATHER OBVIOUSLY LOOKS LIKE)

The
Nuclear Platypus
Biscuit Bible

A Spiritual Guide for the Disciples of Biscuitism

by
Pope Gus Rasputin Nishnabotna
Sni-A-Bar Freak the First

aom

arglebargle omniversal ministry
PUBLICATIONS

"Treading the fine line between exultation and aggression since 1986."

• Being a *belle-lettristic* exposition on the Infinite Glories of the God-Biscuit •

Attention big-shot Hollywood and/or Bollywood producers: Movie rights to *The Nuclear Platypus Biscuit Bible* are currently available. If interested please have your people contact Our people.

Spread thee the word! The publication of *The Nuclear Platypus Biscuit Bible* is the second most important event in all of history, second only to the creation of the universe itself! Please contact the publisher at *nuclear.platypus@god-biscuit.com* if you would like to purchase bulk copies to be left in hotel rooms and at laundromats, or to add the book to your local public school curriculum, &c.

This is a work of *Absolute Universal Reality.* Any resemblance to Cosmic Biscuit Deities living, dead or immortal is coincidental.

God-Biscuit's most sacred vow to thee and thine: For thy protection this Holy Book is guaranteed to be 99.62% free of split infinitives.

No animals, be they real, imaginary, conceptual or mythical, were harmed during the creation of this book.

The Nuclear Platypus Biscuit Bible is available in hardcover, paperback and eBook formats. Coming soon for the functionally illiterate: *The Nuclear Platypus Biscuit Bible: The Fast-Action 'Kwik-Dissolve' Suppository Edition*™ (by prescription only)

ISBN 978-0-578-02663-3   Library of Congress Control #: 2008900551

The
Nuclear Platypus Biscuit Bible
or
There But For The Grace of
God-Biscuit Goes God-Biscuit

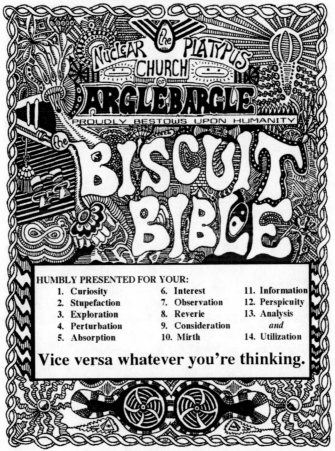

THE NUCLEAR PLATYPUS CHURCH OF ARGLEBARGLE PROUDLY BESTOWS UPON HUMANITY the BISCUIT BIBLE

HUMBLY PRESENTED FOR YOUR:

1. Curiosity	6. Interest	11. Information
2. Stupefaction	7. Observation	12. Perspicuity
3. Exploration	8. Reverie	13. Analysis
4. Perturbation	9. Consideration	*and*
5. Absorption	10. Mirth	14. Utilization

Vice versa whatever you're thinking.

A Saga of Epic Prepostrocity
by
Pope Gus Rasputin Nishnabotna
Sni-A-Bar Freak the First

As seen in the pages of *Popular Mechanics* magazine!

Warning: *The Nuclear Platypus Biscuit Bible* is printed on a special type of retro-reflective paper. This paper was designed by Arglebargle Reality Technicians to reflect light at twice the normal speed, *therefore causing the page to reflect the light before the light even hits the paper.* Due to this curious and counter-intuitive phenomenon it is possible that you will finish reading the book before you even begin, and you could conceivably finish the book *before you ever even look at it.* Indeed, you may have just now read the entire book, which you will not be aware of for days (or even years) to come!

If upon completing your study and analysis of *The Nuclear Platypus Biscuit Bible* you find yourself trapped in an annoyingly relativistic temporal feedback loop, do not panic. Simply avoid any location in which you can reasonably expect yourself to be at the precise moment you're reading this very sentence, and ground yourself by reading about thinking about reading *these three words* at *this precise moment*, and everything will be just fine.

Great Gift Ideas!
• For a small fee of $25,000.00 (plus travel & lodging expenses) Pope Gus himself will perform *The Nuclear Platypus Biscuit Bible* in a five-hour interpretive dance cycle, right in the comfort of your own living room or underutilized backyard gazebo. It's the perfect way to spruce up a BBQ, birthday party or family reunion!

• Purchase a copy of *The Nuclear Platypus Biscuit Bible* for space empires of the distant future! Your extremely remote post-human descendants will struggle through the entropic heat death of the universe in style with the exclusive *Biscuit Bible Deep Future Edition*, encoded in your choice of either base-8 octal or base-16 hexadecimal format and printed on acid-free paper! Only $5,000.00, with Pope Gus's autograph free upon request!

(Vacuum-sealed cryogenic storage module sold separately.)

***This statement has not been evaluated by the
Food and Drug Administration.**

TABLE OF CONTENTS

READ THESE INSTRUCTIONS PRIOR TO USING

• Keep back at least 75 feet (22.86 meters) at all times.
• Not to be read while hang-gliding, as in-flight lapses of concentration leading to serious injury or death may occur.
• *The Nuclear Platypus Biscuit Bible* has been clinically guesstimated to have little discernable effect on gout.
• Shake well before using.
• Reliance upon this book for use as a flotation device during floods or subsequent to zany maritime mishaps is a foolhardy gamble and thus strongly discouraged.
• This sentence appears elsewhere in *The Nuclear Platypus Biscuit Bible*.
• If the reader insists on making that face, the reader hereby acknowledges and accepts the risk that the face in question could conceivably freeze like that.
• Not to be taken internally.
• Following extensive research it has been determined that attempts to gargle this book will leave the reader with an acute sense of dissatisfaction, not to mention papercuts.

The ink used to print this *Commemorative 6,000th Anniversary Edition* is mixed with droplets of actual blood from the Most Holy of Holies, the Mighty Quasi-Mammalian Monotreme of Majesty, the Nuclear Platypus Himself. To keep the earnest seeker of knowledge safe this blood has been tested (1) for communicable diseases; (2) for submission as evidence in immaculate conception-related paternity lawsuits; (3) for organophosphate exposure; (4) for lycanthropism-inducing gene-spliced retroviruses; and (5) for any agents known to cause psoriasis of the liver. Due to the mixture of Nuclear Platypus blood contained herein, the Church of Arglebargle accepts no liability whatsoever in the event that an impulsive reader eats any portion of this book and develops an insatiable craving for the savory and succulent prosciutto-like taste of platypus meat.

FOREWORD

One morning my Yeti-mate Kaosmik Bobcat and I opened our mail to discover, amongst other things, an envelope (day-glo), a short terse note asking for my comments, and a hand-drawn rendition of an ancient Philco television set, on whose screen was scrawled the following cryptic message:

This is your lucky day!
The rest of your life will be compared to today!
You now have in your possession that thing whose essence
exemplifies and defines all things Biscuitoidian!

Overwhelmed as I was by such a bold claim, I immediately began to peruse, in the traditional slack-filled Dobbs-Approved fashion (which is my nature), the contents of the day-glo envelope in which the aforementioned missive was enclosed. In it I discovered the focus of all the attention, *The Nuclear Platypus Biscuit Bible.* It seemed impressive enough with its eye-popping cover and its flashback acid-trip graphics. These features alone were more than enough to cause spasmodic incontinence and Goat Worship in lesser SubGenii.

Then I started to read it. That was either my second greatest mistake or my second greatest achievement, to this day I know not which. Suddenly my eyeballs seized up in their sockets and my brain locked up like the rear end of a '59 Desoto when you shift into reverse at 90 MPH. There I was, looking at the almost indecipherable and obviously coded platitudes of some document *thing* the likes of which I hadn't seen since Moses and I were runnin' buddies. What was this arcane tome of forgotten consciouslessness??

God-Biscuit, Xe8eX, Nuclear Platypus? *What is this stuff?* What's all this gallivanting around the universe and lollygagging with immense omniscient all-powerful deities like some damn demigod of ancient times? Answering questions to which there are no answers? Giving answers to questions not even asked? Did I miss something?

But wait...! Maybe there is something here. This is one of the *weirdest* damn things I've ever run into. It's either the most ridiculous, self-indulgent, cockamamie tripe I've received since the 12th (of never, that is), or some of the most utterly inspired utterances pooted forth by anyone, human or otherwise, maybe even since the time of M'Gleeg, before the days of Yore (and NOT after, as most readers might assume). Only after several unconscious absorptions am I beginning to "get it." Get it?

So what's the birds-eye lowdown on this caper? I mean what *is* the *bottom line*, as bigwig types are wont to say. The *bottom line* is that you've got to actually READ this stuff to get the ultra-secret message that is hypnotically encoded in the letters of the words, *but not the words themselves*. This is the really important part, so remember, *it is not the words that are important*!!! It is the special super-secret Silent Radio™ signal encoding that you hear in your skull at the exact instant that you read *the letters that make up the words*. These words are laden with cabbalistic mysticism and encrypted with subtle subconscious persuasion activators. The very serifs of the letters have more compacted symbolic apocryphal nuances than the Koran or even the works of the venerable T. Lobsang Rampa. It's not the words but the highly religious symbology that permeates each and every letter on the page, independent of the syntax and irrespective of the verbiage contained in the admittedly poetic sentence structure.

And so, Grasshopper, you must be aware that this encoding exists and is there for a purpose, and therefore to propose to your heart to allow the messages to flow into your head like the water flows across the sand and is absorbed thereunto, so to speak, as it were. But enough of my yakkin' already, *read on* and *see* for yourself.

Dr. Philo U. Drummond, Ø1
Overman: First Degree
2nd Authorized MegaFisTemple
Lodge of the Church of the SubGenius
Drummondian-Apostolic

INTRODUCTION

Within the pages of this Holy Book will be revealed to you *everything worth knowing*: the True Nature of All That Is, Was, and One Day Shall Be. Or at least all that is, was, and one day *would* be if anything actually existed, which it doesn't.

I can see that some of you are confused by the previous sentence. It's quite simple really: The universe, "reality" itself, is a sham, a hallucination hallucinated by something that doesn't exist! It's not there!

This is how we know: "Inside" and "outside" are relative concepts. You can't have an "in" side without an "out" side and vice versa, just as you can't have a "back" without a "front," or an "up" without a "down." The existence of one quality depends on the relative nature of its opposite and the differential tension generated therefrom.

Everything that exists is *inside* of a universe, either this one or some other one, which means there is nothing *outside* of a universe. Long-established axioms of logic and relativity dictate that *if there is no outside there can be no inside*, and, of course, no middle. This is incontrovertible proof that nothing exists.

As you read this page I am watching you through a tiny lens embedded in the negative space at the center of this letter **O**; I can see that some of you look bemused, if not outright skeptical. Well I'm not; you can delude yourself if you wish but I'm adamant in my belief that I'm not here, and I am prepared to battle unto the death to assert the fact of my non-existence.

If you spot any errors in this theory it is because the theory does not actually exist, and anything that proves this theory wrong automatically proves that it is right, *ipso facto*.

Now that that's cleared up, read and learn, for herein lie many startling revelations of **Absolute Counterfactual Truth** that would change your life if you existed.

P.S. The fact that you're still reading this shows that, against all logic, you are insistent in your naive belief that you actually exist. Even worse, I now notice that the sheer consensual weight of your erroneous convictions of self-existence has pulled me in too. While I'm "here" I might as well have fun with your façade of apparent reality, so I'll continue writing. Just remember: I am a figment of your imagination and *you are your own imaginary friend.*

Everything is Something.
Nothing is Something.
Everything = Something, and Nothing = Something
Everything = Something = Nothing
Therefore: Everything = Nothing
The members of the Nuclear Platypus Church of Arglebargle
must strive to achieve Nothing at all times.

The goal of *The Nuclear Platypus Biscuit Bible*
is to prove Everything by irrefutably
and incontrovertibly proving Nothing.

CANTO I

BISCUITUS

Herewith describing the golden dawn of the Deity of Dough, the creation of the universe, and the perils of pineapples and government

1   Meanwhile, in the beginning there was nothing. *Really* nothing, like totally, absolutely, truly, really mega-big-time nothing. In fact, it was such maxed-out nothingness that there was not even nothing, it was just an absolute void, a complete lack of nothing.

2   One particular non-eon this lack of nothing was just hanging around doing nothing and being a lack of nothing. Suddenly it realized Its status as a double negative and instantaneously underwent a phase shift, transubstantiating Itself from a lack of nothing to Something. With this tiny quantum hiccup within the universal laws of grammar, the Lack of Nothing, now actually Something, had achieved self-awareness, the old "I think, therefore I think I am (I think)" solipsism schtick.

3   With this realization of self-awareness also came the realization of intense boredom. Something was tired of doing nothing, having nothing, and being Nothing, so It decided to shape Itself into Something attractive and fashionable, yet practical for the Creation of Reality.

4   Something tried to think of something sleek and handsome yet rugged and comfortable, but had no context within which to base Its decisions. And besides, an initial fashion *faux pas* could be forgiven at the outset, considering it was the first time anything had been invented.

5   So ~~lacking any better ideas at the moment~~ in a fit of inspired brilliance it came to pass that the final form the Supreme Being decided to take was that of a fashion-obsessed 24-dimensional hermaphroditic Biscuit with a mild speech impediment (since rectified). Thus **God-Biscuit**, S/He who is the Almighty and Savory Savior, and whose *True and Holy Nickname* is **QUXZBXZBXZB'G'BZXBZXBZXUQ**, proposed Hirself into existence.

6　　With this development God-Biscuit was thrilled by the new possibilities opened before Hir. Alas, S/He then remembered that S/He had created Hirself to be omnisciently all-knowing and all-seeing, so there were no possibilities that S/He didn't already know. So once again S/He was bored.

7　　After a period of thought God-Biscuit realized one thing S/He had never done: S/He had never talked. Then came forth the First Declaration of the God-Biscuit,

> "YEA, THIS SENTENCE THAT I SPEAK, AND
> OF WHICH I SPEAK, 'TIS NOT TRUE."

spake S/He, as the very foundations of Hir irreality quaked from the sonic reverberations and adenoidal-yet-stentorian majesty of Hir voice, and S/He was pleased.

8　　S/He then decided S/He quite enjoyed talking, but alas had no one with whom to talk.

9　　Realizing that talking to oneself too much is a possible sign of mental aberration, God-Biscuit came up with the idea of creating the universe, 24 dimensions of **Absolute Apparent Reality**, as part of Hir divine reality-creation plan, *Operation: Create Someone With Whom To Gossip.*

10　　So it was that on April 30, 14.7 gigabazillion B.C., God-Biscuit blew Hirself up, sending the Yeasty Essence of the Fundamental Cosmic Biscuit in all conceivable directions throughout the polycosm. The expanding cloud of selectrons, squarks and sporks exploded outward in what scientists now call the Big Bang, or, more appropriately, the "Biscuit Bang," or, more accurately still, the *Burstin' Biscuit.*

11　　Thus was the universe created and shaped from the symmetry breakage of the Divine Dough of the God-Biscuit, and lo!, with this development S/He was happy, for S/He would soon have someone to talk to.[1]

---

[1] Plus on the business end of things, as the universe expanded S/He was well positioned to acquire infinite amounts of valuable real estate (and lucrative rental properties) with every passing second.

12   The creation of the universe had a big effect on everything, in much the same way that being born has a big effect on one's life.

SOMETHING GASEOUS THIS WAY COMES

The moment of Creation: God-Biscuit blows Hirself up.
(NOT ACTUAL SIZE)

13   Unfortunately the first day is clouded in mystery, so no one except God-Biscuit knows precisely Whom to blame for what happened. However, sources close to God-Biscuit, who wish to remain anonymous lest they be smote, have provided this previously-classified account:

14   "On the first day God-Biscuit wanted light, but you may recall that S/He had a mild speech impediment, a sort of variant reverse lisp. So when S/He wanted light, instead of saying 'Let there be light,' S/He said 'Let there be *lice*,' and, BEHOLD, there were lice, quadrillions of them permeating the entire cosmos and making it itch something fierce.

15   "S/He looked upon the lice-infested universe and saw that S/He had goofed. After shaving Hir head God-Biscuit converted Hir favorite *Fendi* bag into a bug tent larger than the universe and fumigated reality, using a massive Omega-grade bug bomb to cancel out the lice. Luckily, God-Biscuit articulated Hir words more clearly the second time and BEHOLD there was light, and God-Biscuit looked upon the light and saw that it was good, yadda-yadda, &c. &c.[2]

16   "And lo!, 'twas due to this embarrassing incident that the glorious origin of the universe is shrouded in mystery."

17   God-Biscuit gazed out upon the realm that S/He had created of Hirself and saw that it was good. Even then, though, S/He felt the stirrings of a vague unease that would quickly grow into a problem of colossal magnitude.[3]

18   At the time S/He was so entranced by the sheer joy of pure unmediated existence that S/He chose to cast this unease aside as the side effects of a tough day of universe-building, a sort of mega-hangover from over-twisting the very fabric of space/time.

19   After a few million years of gazing upon the beauty of the as-yet-formless universe, God-Biscuit set about fixing Hir speech impediment and bringing about someone to talk to (and perhaps even text message, if and when evolution finally created opposable thumbs).

20   The first life form other than Hirself whom S/He created was the **Nuclear Platypus**[4], known by many names in many languages, but His true name and title is *The Nuclear Platypus, the Supreme Bean and Most Majestic of All Monotremes.*

21   Next God-Biscuit did create the brothers known as **Quxxxzxxx** and **Quzzzxzzz**. Quxxxzxxx[5] was destined for greatness in later times, becoming a writer and advertising

---

[2] A minor problem at the time being that, before photons were invented, light was composed not of photons but of *beans*, creating a sort of putrid brown plasma that permeated the universe for the first 380,000 years. Finally God-Biscuit got tired of the sickly beanish ambiance and invented photons instead.

[3] Conveniently offering this opportunity to provide dramatic foreshadowing of the admittedly-skimpy plot of the next chapter.

[4] Not to be confused with His hick cousin, the **Nucular Platypus**.

[5] Pronounced *Quxxzxx*, as both the third and fifth Xs are silent, with the emphasis on the second syllable.

mogul responsible for such self-promotional jingles as *Quxxxzxxx: Ask for it by name*, or *You can call me Quxxxzxxx, just don't call me late for dinner*, or *With a name like Quxxxzxxx it's got to be good*. The less said of Quzzzxzzz the better, for he is one of the Secret Archons of the Universe and smites those without clearance to speak His Terrible and Most Holy Name.

22   Quxxxzxxx and Quzzzxzzz occupied themselves by drawing up elaborate business plans, flow charts and finance models to help God-Biscuit and the Nuclear Platypus set up Their assembly line for the creation of more life forms.

23   Shortly thereafter a herd of angels was decanted, hereafter known as **The Doughy Hosts of God-Biscuit**. All in all 5,000 were created to fill the ranks of the Doughy Hosts. Angelic were they, beautiful, noble creatures known as the *Doughish Ones* in the arcane alchemical texts of yore. Aye, blessed they were, corn-fed and well-hydrated, with clear and zit-free skin, flamin' halos, wings like unto the most graceful of swans, perpetual access to the trendiest gadgetry, the most exquisite table manners then available, and mellifluous voices like unto a heavenly choir.

24   Alas, most of the Doughy Hosts died of scurvy, for the omniscient God-Biscuit was then on the Atkins diet and had forgotten to create Vitamin C.[6] Of the 5,000 angels, only the 2,000 strongest and most scurvy-resistant survived. Before they too died off, God-Biscuit invented pineapples, which contained more Vitamin C than anything else in the known universe at that time.

25   Unfortunately, like most no-bid contracts pineapples were plagued by shoddy workmanship, cost overruns and poor design. The end result came out rather violently shaped, covered roundabout with jagged edges and serrated, spiky points; certainly a hazardous and inherently hostile form of fruit if ever there were such a thing.

26   Combine the serious design flaws of the pineapple with the fact that the Doughy Host survivors had (a) become

---

[6] Excusable because, besides Hir *laissez-faire* attitude toward omnipotence, S/He was **literally** making it up as S/He went along.

twitchy with dementia from advanced scurvy; (b) been traumatized by their impending scurvy-induced toothlessness; and, in the midst of the confusion had (c) lost their instruction manuals on how to eat, and it's easy to forecast impending catastrophe.

27 Sure enough, of the 2,000 scurvy survivors another 1,000 were doomed: Having 50/50 odds of randomly choosing the correct major orifice to insert the pineapple into in order to eat it, half made the right choice while half made the wrong choice, thereby mangling themselves beyond recognition or recovery.

Super-Size Me: Oh devoted pilgrim, gaze ye upon the fearsome visage of the Deity of Dough and tremble before Hir majesty!

28 Drastic measures were necessary in order to save the survivors, so on the 7^{11th} day God-Biscuit created oranges.

29 Fortunately, oranges were the necessary key to a happy universe. The members of the Hosts that survived **The Attempted Pineapple-Induced Angelic Genocide**, now spoken of in hushed whispers as *The Unspeakably Gruesome Pineapple Insertion/Ingestion Incident*, went on to live and multiply happily in the paradise that was theirs, having one-sided conversations with the God-Biscuit, Who, being omniscient, always seemed to know what they were going to say next. They lived carefree and even decadent lifestyles, playing hide 'n go seek by themselves, playing drinking games with shot glasses full of Sea-Monkeys, and singing along to disco songs with lyrics like unto, "'Tis the way, uh-huh uh-huh, I like it, uh-huh uh-huh."

30 For the next gazillion years (give or take a few bazillion decades) all was well. Being angels, the Doughy Hosts attempted to come up with suitably Biblical and impressive-sounding speech patterns. However, after a few centuries of saying things like, "I prithee, fain 'twouldst I be were thee, mayhap neither to prattle nor gainsay but simply hie and henceforth to forego strumming thine zither and forsooth peel'st me a grape posthaste," everyone was so neurotically uncertain of whatever-the-heck anyone else was attempting to communicate that the idea was abandoned for more vernacular speech patterns.

31 After the problems with lice and scurvy God-Biscuit took a leave of absence, claiming a need to leave the Hosts to themselves for a while, and to allow the universe to develop without Hir intervention.[7] S/He duly left a sign on the door, and behold, the sign it did say, "Gone fishin'".

32 Over the ages the Hosts had developed their own civilization, complete with denture cream, tummy tucks, strip solitaire tournaments, the most luxurious naugahyde vinyl in all of history, low-carb pasta, celebreality shows, taco night every other Thursday, and government elections every four universal rotations (At the time it took 23,547,921,017 years for the universe to rotate once on its axis; it now takes considerably longer due to universal expansion caused by mid-month galactic bloating, the gravitational effects of nonbaryonic dark matter, and paperclips)[8].

---

[7] Though 'twas rumored that S/He and Hir stunt double had in fact entered rehab to treat Their raging *Chapstick* addictions.

[8] Please refer to 'Appendix VIII: The Horrific Truth About Paperclips, *Revealed At Last*'

33 These quadrennial elections usually brought out the more bombastically self-aggrandizing and arrogant deities like Yahweh, Odin, and Zeus. The deities would insult one another until the voters got fed up and voted for whichever status-seeking sociopath they disliked the least.

34 After the election a statue of the new president would be erected in the park. This was known as the *Presidential Erection* and was the main social event of the season.[9]

35 During one particular election the campaigning was more fierce than usual. The candidates were smiting one another, as was their wont, and Jehovah had just been excommunicated for throwing a temper tantrum and turning Cthulhu into a pillar of salt during a televised debate.

36 Suddenly a new candidate showed up and won a landslide victory, much to everyone's astonishment.

37 After the Inauguration and Presidential Erection everyone realized why they were so astonished: No one knew who this new deity was. This was considered quite strange because usually in a quaint village like Angelopolis everyone knew everyone else.

38 So, 'twas most passing strange that nobody could remember having seen the President before they accidentally elected it. To mystify the electorate even further, it was hard to tell precisely what the President looked like because it always wore a wig and big plastic glasses with a fake rubber nose and mustache attached.

39 At the President's first *State of the Universe* address it began the proceedings by stating authoritatively, "We must deny our femurs before the Nuremberg Pickle!"

40 No one in the audience was quite sure what this meant, but all agreed that, by golly, it sounded like a good idea. The entire crowd surged to its feet applauding wildly, precisely as the focus groups had predicted.

41 Reveling in the masses' adulation, the President paused to adjust its Jeri Curls when suddenly the glasses with

---

[9] The President sometimes left the Presidential Erection early (and quite suddenly, without warning), a frustrating and embarrassing occurrence referred to by the Secret Service as the *Premature Evacuation*.

fake rubber nose and mustache fell off. The crowd erupted into pandemonium upon seeing what the President *really* looked like.

42   With the fake glasses and mustache on as a disguise the President had looked exactly like Shaquille O'Neal,[10] but without the glasses the illusion was dispelled: Where once the President had been there now stood a horrifying kidney-shaped mass of rancid, semi-melted cheese about 42,000.4 millimeters tall, undoubtedly the largest mass of cheese ever to coagulate anywhere in the known universe (up to that time, at least).

43   The cheese pulsated with the Power Cosmic and was covered with huge strips of Velcro, to which were stuck diminutive protomammalian hamster-like organisms in precise Fibonacci spirals like flies on flypaper. Throbbing atop the mass of cheese was an enormous undulating goiter with access to over 6,000 HDTV channels.[11]

44   "Do fish even *like* Cheez Whiz?!?" the President demanded, pounding the lectern and waving lug nuts at the audience as they stampeded out of the auditorium.

45   "Run, you fools! You can't escape from me!" the mass of cheese gurgled, enraged to see its poll numbers and approval ratings plunging dramatically. "Just you wait until I veto a shaved bear with a forty-foot talking lemon!"

46   Just then a giant flaming tree sloth ran across the stage carrying a billboard that said, *"I have no eyelids and must lick my own eyeballs to keep them moist. Call for help."* No one noticed.

47   With a blinding flash, the Nuclear Platypus appeared and confronted the mass of cheese.

48   "What is it that you do here, and who is it that thou doth be?" demanded the Platypus of Power, the Messianic Quasi-Mammal of Might.

49   "I am named **Xe8eX**, the Nephroid of Freeth! I am implementing my plan to usurp the Divine Pretender, that

---

[10] Or perhaps exactly like Donny & Marie Osmond; 'twas a toss-up.
[11] Alas, all 6,000+ were cruddy public access and home-shopping channels.

Biscuitist fool, and claim the throne of Supreme Being for myself. I shall start my reign by ridding myself of you!" said Xe8eX as it slurpily rose up to its mighty height.

50   "Hold on! Wait!" cried the Nuclear Platypus, digging and searching through the pockets of His loincloth.

51   "Ah, here it is... look at this." He said, handing a book to Xe8eX.

52   "What be this?" asked Xe8eX, its voice quaking with wrath as it peristaltically lurched forward with a cockroach-like elegance, eyeing the book warily.

53   "'Tis called **The Nuclear Platypus Biscuit Bible**, universally acclaimed as *the greatest book of all time*. Look; see how chapter two is titled 'The Gospel of the Nuclear Platypus'? We're in chapter one, so if I'm around to write chapter two then obviously you don't kill Me in this chapter."

54   A look of disappointment rippled across Xe8eX's goiter. "I guess that makes sense... but even if I don't kill you I can still be the Supreme Being, can I not?"

55   "Well, let's see...." saith the Nuclear Platypus, His flipper flipping quickly through the pages.

56   "Nope. Even at the end of the book it's still 'God-Biscuit,' not 'God-Xe8eX.' It looks like after 171 words from now you play no further role in the rest of the book, or universe. In fact, skimming ahead it seems that near the end of the next paragraph you slip and fall into a split infinitive and are never heard from again, other than a few brief mentions here and there, but those don't really count. Sorry."

57   Turning slowly, the mass of semi-coagulated cheese slithered away liquescently, slobbering and gurgling its despondency to any and all who would listen. The oleaginous megalomaniac lurched along slowly in order to make this, the last paragraph in which it mattered, last *just that much longer*, struggling valiantly to make every word, every phoneme, count. Hoping at least to see its name in print just one last time, and possibly even emphasized in italics and underlined, *Xe8eX* solemnly noted that the paragraph was winding down to these final 29 words and so chose to sadly give in to the inevitable and, like a candle in the wind, deliquescently disappeared and was never heard from thereafter.

58   After a while the Hosts decided that the concept of government was just a passing fad and everybody forgot about it, settling back into the quotidian rhythms of everyday existence.

59   All was well with the universe again as God-Biscuit peeked back in to check on the status of reality. Casually dressed to the nines with *Lucky Brand* jeans cut into Daisy Dukes, shoes by *Buster Brown*, a blouson tank top from *Anthropologie* and a hoodie from *Phat Farm*, S/He showered Hir Doughish Hosts with Hir Eternal Doughy Love. The Doughish Ones in turn daily thanked Hir for the paradise S/He had created of Hirself as their natural habitat.

60   Unbeknownst to the Hosts, however, the vague sense of unease that God-Biscuit had felt since paragraph **17** had grown to an all-powerful premonition of fear and uncertainty.

61   As God-Biscuit scanned the heavens searching for the cause of the disturbance, Hir all-knowing and all-seeing omnipotence could not penetrate one specific sector of the universe, not even with the aid of the designer X-ray specs S/He had bought from *Van Cleef & Arpels* at Fifth and 57th.

62   This area, where the Earth's solar system would one day form, was home to a binary star system with 17 planets, and was even then a focal point for energies in the universe. But now all was quite quiet, the area shielded somehow and thus completely resistant to God-Biscuit's probing curiosity. Lacking in actionable intelligence, Hir disquiet continued to grow.

63   S/He then realized that part of Hir unease was the result of caffeine overload. S/He noted that reality was positively *drenched* in caffeine, and that the members of the Hosts were complaining of the jitters, insomnia, twitchiness, diuresis and acute psychomotor agitation. God-Biscuit realized that this universal caffeine permeation was somehow related to the appearance of the dark sector of reality, so S/He decided S/He had no choice but to investigate.

64   However, it's hard to move around within objective reality when you *are* objective reality, so S/He called upon the Nuclear Platypus to save the day, to move like the solar winds and discover what lurked within the dark sector.

65 With that, the Nuclear Platypus donned His sombrero and prepared Himself for this, His mission of missions. Amid much hoopla, fanfare, and a *fin de siècle* high-steppin' doo-wop trip-hop bhangra bebop calypso/merengue hoompah hoedown ragtime nerdcore jamboree, He was off to meet His destiny, blissfully unaware of the horror that awaited Him.

THE EIGHT PRIMARY TRIGRAMS OF THE BISCUITIST REALITY STRUCTURE

WE HOLD THIS DOUGH TO BE SELF-BAKING:
Rights endowed by the Creator should include the right to keep and eat fruit.

The above diagram depicts the sub-Planck scale format of reality itself. Broken down for purposes of clarity into the constituent granular and wavicular components that weave the mesh of reality, the cosmogluten-based elements shown above manifest as quantum loops, eggplants, superstrings, quarks, sporks, entropy-distributing processes & *aardvarks-in-potentia*.

CANTO II

THE GOSPEL
OF THE
NUCLEAR PLATYPUS

Herewith narrating the valiant struggle of the forces of
righteousness against the Anti-Biscuit

1   Rage: Muse, sing thee the rage of God-Biscuit's own,
        the Nuclear Platypus,
        murderous, flatulent; with flippers and a duckbill
        most cartilaginous,
        hurling down to Hell a mass of melted cheese quite
        mucilaginous,
        slimy and cheesy, its skin covered with mold most
        oleaginous,
        greasily lurching forth, quite aborborygmatous —

2   Er, hey, that red light thingie is flashing; wait, the
recorder is already on? Oh. Oops... how embarrassing. [—
grumble (inaudible) —] All right, let's start over... Uh,
'*Unless Jack and Jill whacked the pupa with a mallet, they*
ran a terrible risk that Jill's ruptured —' Wait, that's the
wrong book... hold on, here we go. Gimmie a second...

3   [—*ahem* —]

4   Know ye now that what thou dost read is the inspired
word of I, who am the Nuclear Platypus, the Supreme Bean
and Most Majestic of Quasi-Mammalian Monotremes.

5   In the beginning was the Void, and from the Void
came that Biscuit that is the Lack of the Void, the
Absolutized Absence of Nothing, the Blessed Biscuit from
which the universe itself is come.

6   From that Biscuit came the Word, and the Word is
the sound of a glorious Biscuit that is the All in Each, and the
Word is thus truthfully spake as this:

The Twelve Commandments of the God-Biscuit

I.   Thou shalt not obey this commandment.

II.   A watched phone never boils.

III.   Everybody Wang Chung Tonight.

IV.   Always wear clean underwear, in case thou art in an accident and must go to the hospital.

V.   The following sentence, 'tis false.

VI.   The previous sentence, 'twas true.

VII.   Runneth ye not while holding scissors.

VIII.   Put thou thine drink on a coaster post-haste, before thou dost ruin the mahogany veneer.

IX.   Vice versa whatever thou art thinking.

X.   Fryest thee not thine bacon whilst thou art naked.

XI.   Say it, don't spray it.

XII.   Thou shall bake no other Gods before Me.

+ free bonus Commandment![12] (for a limited time only, void where prohibited by slaw)

XIII.   Thou shalt *think not* of a cheeseplug.

7   And such was the Word spake unto Me for all the cosmos to behold on the day that I did leave My home to discover what lurked within the Dark Sector of reality.

8   It was now when first I left, and the faster I went the rounder I got. Setting the controls for the heart of the sun I traveled at excessive speed, zipping along at eleventy-seven times the speed of space, and BEHOLD: I moved *too* fast and (literally) got ahead of Myself, accidentally arriving at My destination before I had even departed.

9   'Twas most irritating: Because I had not yet left I wasn't there, but because I had already arrived I *was* there; I was there yet I was not, and vice versa. Among the many ontological and epistemological quandaries this caused was the nearly insurmountable problem of trying to figure out *what to pack* for such a peculiar, subjectively paradoxical and temporally bifurcated set of circumstances.

---

[12] To make it a straight baker's dozen.

The Nuclear Platypus

10   I decided that when finally I caught up with Myself or vice versa, Myself and I should promptly contemplate starting over in order to avoid any unnecessary confusion between Myself and/or Me and/or I. Exhausted by trying to keep track of Myselves, I said My evening prayer[13] and went to sleep for the night.

---

[13]   "Now I lay Me down to sleep
I pray God-Biscuit, My Dough to keep
If My Dough should fry before it bakes
I guess 'tis doughnuts instead that I shall make
Amen."

11   Like Parzival on his quest I did travel long and far, more slowly this time, for well-nigh a fortnight of interstellar overdrive. Barely stopping to rest, I traversed over 187.2 trillion furlongs (as the crow flies), racking up some truly righteous airline miles, and all was fine at the first.

12   As I traveled onward I passed a series of quasars emblazoned with a *Burma Shave* jingle:

Rubbery, unshaven platypus duckbill
With fibrous whiskers so rough,
Your webbed flippers look silly to me
You're not so tough.
Burma Shave.

13   This I found most disturbing, for besides the crude hand-lettering painted by the obviously arthritic hand of an illiterate brute, a quick check of My itinerary indicated that Burma Shave was not to be invented for some three-score zillions of years. An obvious forgery, the sign was a most slanderous assault upon My person.

14   As if being subject to potentially litigious libels weren't bad enough, from behind the final Burma Shave sign erupted a police cruiser, lights flashing and siren wailing. 'Twas a Smokey on My tail, and I was the victim of the first known speed trap in the history of the universe!

15   I pulled over and a spindly Fife-like organism named **Prunus Guster** came sauntering up to Me, ticket book in hand. The overzealous constabulary beamed the "Green Acres" theme song directly into the dorsal surface of My electroreceptive snout with a potentially conceptual bagpipe, and then proceeded to cite Me for a broken "tail" light. The nerve!

16   Closer and closer I came to the Dark Sector, and My unease continued to grow. One morning I had just broken down camp, finished My morning bowl of *Purina Platypus Chow*, emptied My chamber pot and folded up My doily when I noticed My hoss Sleipnir was most distressed. I heard a strange rustling sound over yonder by the hitchin' post when suddenly a five-ton monstrosity, half-dingo, half-stoat, half-cabbage and half-jellyfish, lurched out from behind the cacti. Revolting in its goitrogenic cruciferousness and armed with a chain saw, it belched up enormous quantities of bleach and mustard as it gargled its own urine in a manner most uncouth. Wishing to avoid a confrontation with such a beast, I fooled the pugnaciously gelatinous and herbaceous dingo-stoat thing into pulling My flipper and disappeared posthaste, camouflaged in a lavender cloud of platypus flatulence.

17 Many perils have I faced to defend the glory of the God-Biscuit, and never once did I feel the icy touch of fear; not when I faced down the blueberry-embedded blasphemy of the messianic **Muffin Master**[14], nor when dire circumstance forced Me to aerate the fetid underpants of **Gerbilax the Drippy**.

18 This time, however, was different, and everything was subtly changed in a manner most difficult to discern.

19 For one thing, I felt as if unseen forces were sniffing My every move. 'Twas at this point I noticed that My arm flippers and leg flippers had switched positions with one another. This was rather unprecedented, and My new body configuration stressed considerably the tailoring of My loincloth, bursting seams, popping grommets and leaving Me victim to extensive and uncomfortable chafing.

20 I traveled thus for a few days, hoping none of My friends would happen to see Me in such an awkward and delicate condition, and then discovered that I could return to My normal self if I yanked on My tongue while talking inside out, like so:

21 I eledyod lachianAppa oet-perstap ni wardsback igP tinLa nda adh na geur ot injo gEg-tersBea ymousAnon.

22 While distracted by some in-depth solitary nasal-mining explorations, I discovered that I had crossed the penumbra and was within the Dark Sector already; I had come upon it unawares.

23 My body shivered and quaked from massive caffeine overload, besieging Me with a fierce case of the vapors as reality took on a languidly frantic Pepto pink pallor.

---

[14] Upon autopsy the Muffin of Mayhem was found to have a vanilla cream-filled center, and was thus quite obviously some sort of nightmarish muffin/Twinkie hybrid.

24 Suddenly My body froze, and from above Me came a sound unlike any I had ever heard, like a washing machine full of peanut butter falling down a water slide. At first I thought it was a nasal hallucination, but then I saw a sight that I shall remember for all the rest of My days:

25 There It was like a quivering, bronze-covered artificially-inseminated eggplant with a hailstorm in It. It had the trunk of an elephant, the tentacles of an octopus, and with Its spatulate, prehensile toes It was walking on stilts. Instead of eyelids that open and shut like normal, Its eye sockets opened and closed like beady little sphincters, twisting open and dilating to reveal the seething rage within Its puckered, bulging pupils.[15] Deeply embedded in Its leathery forehead was an ingrown fungus-covered toenail with a banner emblazoned with the clichéd motto *I myself would rather eat grease with Jesus in Central America.* Its distended body was clothed in a positively hideous ensemble of overalls, mismatched plaids, fishnet stockings, rubber waders, and woefully inappropriate thong underwear that barely covered Its swollen rump, which was greasy and glistening and purple like unto that of a monkey in heat, and from which was dribbling a sludgy substance streaked with oily blue veins of mold, like a fine Roquefort cheese. Below the bottom of the top of Its head were 16,719,323 bandicoots massed in a shotgun formation to spell out, "Hairless! Imploding!" A propeller beanie was perched atop Its acromelic and megacephalous head in a pathetic attempt to hide the greasy comb-over that topped Its mullet most dreadful.

26 With dripping paintbrush in palsied hand, this was obviously the dastardly perpetrator behind the fraudulent (not to mention potentially litigable) Burma Shave sign. Verily forsooth, My nemesis was on the premises!

27 Via the conceptual bagpipe that Prunus Guster had used, It turned and said unto Me, "Little thing, what be you doing in my domain, the humble homestead of myself?"

28 Outraged that It had deigned to speak unto Me as if just some commoner were I, I did say, "Ask not of Myself!

---

[15] 'Twas totally gnarly unto the max.

What dost *ye* do behind a veil of secrecy that even the God-Biscuit Hirself cannot penetrate? From whither and whence dost one such as ye come? Name thineself and tell Me of the foul deeds that thou wouldst perpetrate without the consent of the Almighty Deity of Dough!"

**Experience the joys of Universal Destruction!
Thrill to scenes of Caffeinated Universal
Vibratory Annihilation!**
Witness the end of "reality" as we know it!
Rated Ω
COMING SOON TO A UNIVERSE NEAR YOU

29   "Little thing, thou knowest not whom ye order about so callously. I am evil incarnate. Aye, am I the **Anti-Biscuit!** Verily doth I be known by that most fearsome name, that of **The SpapOopGannopOlop**, and I am not of this reality!" saith the SpapOopGannopOlop, nefariously twirling Its handlebar mustache.

30   Just then a tiny mass of gigantic inflatable peat moss fell out of Its barnacle-encrusted mouth and hurtled towards Me in slow motion, flickering like unto low-budget stop-motion animation. I tried to move but My body was frozen by the will of the SpapOopGannopOlop. Fortunately the inflatable peat moss popped before it hit Me and frizzled off to and fro into the nothingness of space.

31   "Now dost thou witness the sheer awesomosity of my powers!" spake the SpapOopGannopOlop as It revolved down into the sky and hovered mere cubits in front of Me.

32   "I shall make you rue the day that ever you dared to confront the SpapOopGannopOlop, who dislikes vegetarians and doth be irritated by the metric system!

33   "As for the deeds that I have in store, this universe, *your universe*, has upset the balance of *my universe*, within which *I* am Supreme Being. To remedy the pernicious effects of your reality I have come to convert all of the hydrogen, *the most abundant form of matter in your universe*, into caffeine. As a result, your entire reality will be totally wired and will twitchily vibrate itself out of existence!"

34   "Blasphemer!" yelleth I, "We shall see how your plan fares when I inform the God-Biscuit of it, once I have finished you Myself!"

35   "Ah, but you shant do that, now shall you?" It said, as Its undulating umbilical cord transformed into a dreadfully unkempt two-toed salamander that began crushing Me most painfully. I tried to resist but was, alas, no match for a life form of the SpapOopGannopOlop's fearsome power.

36   Just as I was ready to give up the ghost there was a blinding flash, the squeal of screeching tires, and a brief, inspirational snippet from the 1960s *Batman* TV show theme song. And lo!, I did see the sartorial splendor of the Glory of Glories: the God-Biscuit Hirself, emerging from behind the wheel of the *Pontiac* BiscuitMobile, flinging aside *D&G* shades with a flourish, Hir *Burberry* scarf fluttering in the solar wind. Adding to Hir fabulous majesty were pinstriped trousers from *Prada*, green chinos from *J.Crew*, a trilobite-encrusted push-up brassiere from *Fredericks of Hollywood*, an ascot from *Hermés*, racing gloves from *Hugo Boss*, cufflinks by *Coach*, flip-flops from *Dress Barn* and scent by *Dior*. S/He was in a fighting mood and quite obviously ready for some heavy-duty Yeast-Flingin.'

37　　Fireworks erupted, backlighting the God-Biscuit's chitinous *Armani* exoskeleton and illuminating product placements for Hir latest start-up company, *I Can't Believe It's Not Gristle*-brand gristle substitute (now with three times the crunch!).

38　　With Mine own ears I didst hear Hir voice, and yea that voice It did say, "At this point I still appear to be Me. Whether this is a good sign remains to be seen, for *I am The Biscuit That Is God!*"

39　　"God-Biscuit!" I cried, My fusion reactors pulsating with joy to be in Hir golden, crusty presence again.

40　　"What doest you here, thou meddling doughball?!?" screameth the SpapOopGannopOlop.

41　　And the lord God-Biscuit gazed upon Me and smiled from within Hir pleochroic halo. Then S/He turned Hir mighty visage upon the SpapOopGannopOlop and saith: "Now, you who be called the Spap-Oop-Gannop-Olop, the OopGannop of SpapOlop, aye verily the OopOlop of the SpapGannop, now you shall learn to appreciate the concept of the Argarbonzo, that which means 'How to affect your Scandinavian cesspool!'"

42　　The sky turned inside out and a chorus of epileptic aardvarks began chanting in Morse code backwards. My entire being was torn apart and restructured as the God-Biscuit and the SpapOopGannopOlop faced off, trading cosmos-rattling blows. The SpapOopGannopOlop swung Its stilts wildly through the air, trying to whack God-Biscuit as if S/He were some Doughy piñata, and frantically spritzing aerosol *Dough-B-Gon* into the air. God-Biscuit, using moves S/He had learned during careful study of *Soul Train* reruns, zipped hither and thither and to and fro, floating like unto a butterfly and stinging like unto a bee, and squirting out Doughballs that smacked the SpapOopGannopOlop in the face, enraging It further.

43　　Upon the cosmic balance, the mighty scale of the *Infinite Love of the God-Biscuit* vs. *the Caffeinated Wrath of* *the SpapOopGannopOlop* teetered precariously, ready to tilt all of Creation back into the nothingness that once had reigned, as unto a mirror shattered in formless reflections of matter.

44   As I stood there quaking from caffeine overload, My senses reeling from the clash of the two leviathans, directly to My left appeared scores of self-vomiting sea cucumbers. Each self-vomited sea cucumber was thinking about rows of corncobs, which they then proceeded to gather into Penrose-Richert tessellations to perform the Heimlich maneuver on a herd of prolapsed dicynodonts in slow motion.

45   Slowly, voluptuously, the prolapsed dicynodonts did coalesce into a totally enormous phosphorescent frog, and behold!, the sea cucumbers disappeared one by one in tiny little vomitous biophoton bursts.

46   Eyes agog with befuddlement, the God-Biscuit and the SpapOopGannopOlop turned away from one another and ceased their battle. The SpapOopGannopOlop asked, "Who else doth come to meddle in these affairs?"

47   The totally enormous phosphorescent frog answered, croaking, "I be the **Paradise Frog**! I am the X-factor at the nexus of all realities from across the omniverse. Yea, the unpredictable intermediary am I, the Supreme Avatar of Militant Agnosticism (not to mention the Lord of Grits). Alongside you two, I am one-third of the *Trinity of All-Powerful Entities*, completed by the SpapOopGannopOlop as evil and by the God-Biscuit as good. And, lest you forget, I am also the Zumigaltous of the Colmizarious!"[16]

48   "You are naught more than a troublesome toad of indecision to one such as I!" saith the SpapOopGannopOlop. "Begone with you, 'ere I transport you back to my domain. There you shall live e'er in the shadow of agony, for there one lives on a diet containing *little or no roughage*, keeping one miserably constipated for all eternity! Bwah-ha-ha!"

---

[16] The Zumigaltous is an arcane aspect of Gnostic Biscuitism that humanity must *never* discover, for fairly obvious reasons. The Colmizarious doubly so.

49 "Thou knowest as well as I that thou possesseth not the power required to do such a thing," saith the Paradise Frog, hopping closer to the two combatants.

50 "You, I, and the God-Biscuit are equals in every respect. 'Twas hoped that we three would never need meet, but the winds of fate have blown us together. Let us be done with this, for I, like any overscheduled Supreme Being, have things to do and sinners to smite.

51 "I shall be the mediator, the decisive factor in this dispute. Ponder what I say, for 'tis beyond doubt the most significant words ever anyone hath spake! **The Ultimate, Absolute Secret of All Reality**, *never before revealed* and *never to be repeated* is—

PLEASE STAND BY...

We interrupt this bible for an important Public Service Announcement sponsored by Noggin Barn, *your friendly neighborhood phrenology emporium:*
GOD-BISCUIT HAS TEMPORARILY LOST HIR WEATHER PERMIT, SO THERE WILL BE NO WEATHER TODAY. TOMORROW, HOWEVER, IT WILL BE OVERCAST OR CLEAR, DRY OR WET, HOT OR COLD OR ANY COMBINATION THEREOF, AND/OR SOMEWHERE IN BETWEEN. FOR THAT MATTER, IT MAY EVEN BE SOME ALTERNATE POSSIBILITY HERETOFORE UNDREAMT; IT'S REALLY TOO EARLY TO TELL AND BESIDES, THESE THINGS CAN BE PRETTY COMPLICATED TO PREDICT. REGARDLESS, WE NOW RETURN YOU UNTO THE REGULARLY SCHEDULED BOOK OF RELIGIOUS PROPAGANDA.

"—and *that* is the dread secret!" said the Paradise Frog.

52 "I say thee nay!! I shall not abide!" screeched the SpapOopGannopOlop, startled, as were We all, by the magnitude of the incredible secret just revealed. "Better that I swallow myself than believe something so amazing!"

53 "Enough!" said the God-Biscuit and the Paradise Frog at several speeds simultaneously.

54 "If thou will abideth not by the Paradise Frog's ruling, then what happens next is of thine own making!" saith the God-Biscuit, self-harmonizing at 33, 45 and 78 rpm.

55 Then, exactly 1.4 billionths of 6.1 trillionths of $1/1,000^{th}$ of a jiffy before the SpapOopGannopOlop could respond, the God-Biscuit and the Paradise Frog merged into the **Rudimentary Kumquat**. Seething with the unfettered cosmic energies of Basic Is-ness, they absorbed the nearby binary star-system and sprouted luxurious locks of hair from every pore and concavity of the kumquat's pulpy and flaccid body.

NOT the Paradise Frog: 'Tis the BooHoo Frog, close friend and *Iditarod* partner of both King Solomon's Frog and Jeremiah the Bullfrog, and the Paradise Frog's tax advisor's uncle's fourth cousin thrice removed.

56   As the SpapOopGannopOlop looked on transfixed in abject disbelief, the Kumquat, a fully dimensionless point of *Something-Almost-But-Not-Quite-There*, did collapse inward upon Itself in a fluctuating display of gamma radiation and crystallized protein-based follicles. A nose-lute materialized and played either Beethoven's Ninth Symphony or "I'm My Own Grandpaw" by Homer & Jethro, spliced in with the phlegmy gurgles of some sort of dehydrated, raspily-panting marsupial; 'twas hard to tell which due to all the noise kicked up by the nearby Wagnerian cosmic ruckus.

57   With the spontaneous implosion of the Kumquat there did open **The Groined Vault of Infinity**, afflicting the SpapOopGannopOlop with a *Maximized Crypto-Wedgie* and transporting It back to Its corresponding reality.

58   As the SpapOopGannopOlop was set to motion in the unbecoming, spinning round about *The Swirling Vortex of*

That-Biscuit/Frog-That-Is-A-Kumquat, Its beady, sphincterish eyeballs were clenched in grimaces of absolute rage.

59 "Mark thee mine words! 'Tis but a temporary victory on your part! Beware thou the Mutated Bovine Quadrupeds[17], who would rain AIDS-causing doughnuts upon thee![18] Within them shall linger my everlasting legacy!

60 "When next someone doth speak my fearsome name **BACKWARDS,** *ON ACCIDENT*, then shall I, the very SpapOopGannopOlop Itself, return! Only then wilt thou truly experience the Caffeinated Wrath of I, whom art me, myself; then wilt thou learn the fearsome and shocking truth about paperclips!"[19]

61 And behold, the SpapOopGannopOlop was gone, blinked out with the Paradise Frog and the God-Biscuit, returned to their respective states of being. The conclusion of the battle, henceforth known in legend as the *Argle Froggle Spapple*, had happened so quickly that it was over almost before it began.

62 Light was cast upon the Dark Sector for the first time in ages. The binary star-system that once was there had been destroyed; already the residual energies of the old stars were merging with the burnt-out carcass of the kumquat, starting the process that would one day culminate in the star-system Sol and its planets.

63 Though I had been a mere bystander, I felt changed by the battle. The nature of good and evil had been altered in some subtle way, hovering at the very edge of perceptibility. It had been destined to happen since before the dawn of time,

---

[17] Please refer to 'Appendix VIII: The Horrific Truth About Paperclips, *Revealed at Last*'

[18] There is a large body of circumstantial evidence suggesting that doughnuts cause AIDS, the most persuasive argument being that before there were doughnuts, there were no reported cases of AIDS, but now that there *are* doughnuts, there is also AIDS. Coincidence?? *Not likely.* (The proposed etiology is admittedly complex, so the possibility that AIDS causes doughnuts is also being investigated.)

[19] Please refer to 'Appendix VIII: The Horrific Truth About Paperclips, *Revealed at Last*'

and now the first cycle of the Meeting of the Trinity had
come to its stunning *denouement*.

64   I felt not bad for having played only a bit part in this
cosmic drama, for 'twas destined to be beyond My scope, for
a God-Biscuit I am not. I am but second to one such as S/He,
for I am the Nuclear Platypus, verily.

Counter-counterclockwise from top left: The Mighty RevRalph,
Pope Gus Rasputin Nishnabotna Sni-A-Bar Freak the First, and
Rev. Name-Withheld-By-Request discuss matters of importance
that will profoundly affect the lives of bazillions of Church
members across the wounded galaxies.

INTERREGNUM:
AND NOW, A WORD FROM OUR SPONSORS

EAT! EXCRETE! IT'S NEAT!

<u>NOTE</u>: PLEASE CALL 24 HOURS IN ADVANCE IF YOU WISH TO HAVE YOUR MEAL PRE-MASTICATED BY ONE OF OUR CERTIFIED BICUSPULAR HOMODONTIC CHEWING EXPERTS.

ENTREES:

<u>Self-Digesting Pasta</u>: A self-perpetuating form of linguine that eats itself, excretes itself, and then eats itself again. It sure looks tasty, but don't try to eat it because it enjoys eating itself and hates when someone else tries to get in on the action. Trust us: *You don't want something sliding down your throat if it's mad at you.* Collectors' item retractable backup mini-esophagus available on request, just in case.

<u>Invisible Corn</u>: The masses demand the Puckered Alien, but the Puckered Alien demands Invisible Corn! It doesn't look completely unlike anything you've never seen before, but pretty close! We suspect this invisible self-lubricating vegetable to be the root of language!

<u>Dead Bat In A Jar of Peanut Butter</u>: Open the jar and react with gaping horror as jolts from implanted electrodes cause the bat to quiver and twitch within its protein-laden hell in a gooey, grotesque parody of life.

<u>Scabs 'n Hair</u>: Bad things happen when you chew it. Munch all you want, we'll pick more!

<u>Kentucky Raw Unchicken</u>: Delicious; tastes nothing like chicken because it isn't chicken, hence the name 'unchicken'. Certainly not meat, and barely even meat-like, but definitely *meatesque.* Served at the peak of rawness.

<u>Triple-Action Peanut Envy</u>: We got it. You want it.

<u>Blushin' Pork Chop</u>: If you tell it intimate secrets then waves of subtle color palpitate across it as the pork chop blushes. Hey baby, let's meat!

<u>Pan-Scorched Gerbil Dippers</u>: A sampler platter piled high with our ho-made Swamp Flounder Squishies, the Emergent Meatloaf Popsicle, Floppy Nuggets, Stretch Loaf, Pork Lumps, Tuna-Loops, Meat Berries, Double-Dipped Chunk-Style Scab Flaps, Pork Log Delight, Hair Slaw, Diet Gnorple,

Crawfish Wipers, the Prune-Flop Surprise!, Fleas 'n Peas, and freshly-severed Meat Stinkies. They're *gerbilicious*!

A Talking, Screaming Kidney Stone: I scream, you scream, Quing screams for a Talking, Screaming Kidney Stone! Quing is not responsible for a bereft palate. $2.00.

The Space Between Food: The perfect meal for those who watch their weight. No fat, no sodium, no calories, no spatial location. For instance, instead of eating fat-laden potato chips you eat the fat-free space *between* the potato chips. Not even the schoolyard bully can steal the space between food.

Edible Vaseline: Scrumptious, oily and nearly-edible egg-flavored paste. Keeps small invertebrates from trying to crawl into your mouth. Seedless, add $0,000,000.00.

Analog Corndog: Much less overtly hostile than its digital predecessor. Due to vehement customer demand we've surgically removed those sucker-paw things.

The Accidental Turnip: The world's most suitable pay-per-view vegetable! Generally quite compatible with human-style organisms. *Caution*: May contain ingredients.

Refried Ectoplasm: Freshly harvested from the pineal gland of a Venusian swamp cucumber!

Thing Full of Stuff: You can participate in activities with it.

Pucumber: Busted by Aunt Jemima while trying to cross the border with a suitcase full of lizard dandruff; snagged in a thistle bush in someone's front yard, delirious and sticky with sweat; genitalia rubbed raw and bleeding from an unnatural outbreak of BBQ beef sandwiches; abducted by space aliens and forced to undergo a routine dental examination. Suddenly, along comes a duck. In the duck's bill, yours for the taking, is Pucumber, the vomit vegetable!

The Deep-Fried Boneless Chicken Beast: A meal fit for a Quing! It is hovering in the hot summer night, reminding me of you. Exudes a hearty, meat-like aroma.

Meat Blanket: Put some pep in your step with the most Freudian form of food ever! We encase you in a hot, sticky cocoon of raw beef. The atmosphere inside grows increasingly dank and smelly. Your eyes dart to and fro as claustrophobia sets in. Your air supply is running out! Thrashing about wildly, your desperation becomes so great that you chew your way out, savoring the hickory-smoked flavor of survival! Now in convenient aerosol spray can form!

Inflatable Peanut Butter: Yum! Tastes like a dog-whistle sounds. Lollipop with egg-yolk center, add, $1.09.

Squid Ink Surprise: Bring your own pasta and we'll provide an easily-antagonized squid strapped into a leather S&M bondage harness!

Wartloaf: A fine deli platter piled high with tasty lunchmeat subjected to intense radiation fields. The meat mutates, growing tumors, boils and chewy warts, providing that much sought-after sensation of pimples exploding in your mouth! Real good eatin', and the best source of roughage since our legendarily crunchy cockroach jamboree.

Tickloaf: A 2.5 cubits long, by 1.5 cubits wide, by 1.5 cubits thick loaf of sourdough bread with ticks and chiggers baked in. Sometimes them little critters survive the baking process! A healthy combo of complex carbohydrates and chitinous protein. Voted *Official Chigger of the 1521 Diet of Worms.*

Ho-Made Beings 'n Weenies: Neither organic nor inorganic, natural nor artificial, this food merely *is.* Belches up large clouds of dust as it vibrates through your table. Though troublesome to dogmatic Aristotelians, this remains the favorite food of Rudolph Bhegga.

Chunk o' God-Biscuit: Exists at every wavelength of every spectrum, defying definition. Guaranteed to overload and short out all five senses, plus ones you don't even have yet!

Clapper-Activated Cream Corn: Amidmost the lentils, a basic principle of manginess, an enema enigma. The best thing to come along since Sir Isaac Newton discovered gravy. $.09.

Mold McMuffin: Eating this is like reliving memories of things you've never done. Somehow eludes detection by all five senses. You can occasionally glimpse it asquint from the corner of your eye, but usually you can observe it in its natural habitat only when you don't look at it. May cause retroactive birth defects. Mungball, add $125.00.

Meat with a 'Pause' Button: It's more than just an object! Trying to determine the precise physical nature of this interactive gustatory delight will unnerve you and your colleagues well into the wee hours of the morn. Is it some form of extinct primate covered with green feathers? Or is it a long clump of hair tied at both ends, ready to be dipped in meat sauce? Or are the rumors true, and it's a prehistoric hybrid of a fish and jalapeño pepper, a relic delicacy from eons long past before fish and jalapeño peppers branched off from the same genetic tree, with a look like a scaly pepper with gasping gills and a tail? According to the Copenhagen Interpretation it's up to you! Tunnel Turkey, $-127.54 extra.

Sexually Transmitted Hamburgers: Yum! Our chef's favorite food since before birth! Quing piles the food high atop a pendulum swinging in a giant, cavernous, and soundproofed dungeon. Your hands tied behind your back, you will run frantically back and forth, screaming between bites and catching chunks of chalky gristle and stringy meat as centrifugal force flings it against dank, lichen-covered granite walls crawling with dung beetles, their iridescent carapaces glittering prismatically in the twilight, refining and clarifying the visceral horror of your situation. The meat will mix with your stomach acid and flow back up your throat, your tongue will blister, you will have seizures and pass out from exhaustion, but no matter how hard you work and how much you eat you will never have enough. *Bon appétit*! Only $1.25, plus signed, notarized consent form.

U.F.O. (Unidentified Frying Object): It's Meast, the Meat Beast! We dare you to lick it! $1.00, cash on the barrelhead.

Primordial Soup: A convenient dehydrated soup for lunch on the go. Just add water, carbon and deoxyribonucleic acid, microwave it and you've got life! Eat it quick before it evolves the means to defend itself and fight back.

The Meat Stall: Not a food but a location. The perfect place to wear bologna as a tree stump impersonates you for three years. Primate compatible, $2.00 extra.

418 Senior Citizens Shouting At A Circular Block of Cheese With A Flag Sticking Out of the Top of It: Self-explanatory and batter-fried with gravy. $1.00, adjusted for deflation.

Kids' Gravel Meal: Children enjoy it more than they enjoy peeling off their skin and lounging around in a bathtub full of skunk pus on a hot summer day! No longer includes the ubiquitous Multiple Monkey Mound, which has apparently escaped,[20] but frequently features the notorious Marshmallow Wedgie for only $.75 extra.

DESSERTS:

Candide Apples: For today's on-the-go fetishistic hominid.

Fur-Flavored Inside-Out Cake: A delicious texture-flavored dessert. Our special mixing method causes this cake to invert spontaneously, thus occupying all available space in the universe except that space in which the cake exists.

The Tiny Mouse-With-A-Human-Ear-On-Its-Back: It drinks 87 cups of coffee every day so its babies will be born without feet! Please donate $1.00.

Picklecicle: Fresh-squeezed pickle juice frozen and molded into the shape of your favorite cartoon character impaled on a stick. Woe be unto those who deign to stick their tongues out afterward.

Bacon Yogurt: We guarantee it probably won't stare at you lasciviously from across the table, winking and undulating.

Squid Muffin: Sprays the room with inky darkness when bitten into. Our patented baking method keeps muffin movement to a minimum. Extremely unnatural. $.79.

BEVERAGES:

Verbal Tea: A refreshing beverage for those intent on categorizing all sensory stimulation into rigidly defined semantic structures. Like trying to drink a squirrel buried under a mound of mashed potatoes.

Tuna Schnapps: A thick, syrupy fish-flavored alcoholic libation certain to make you stumble around, act stupid and say things you will later come to regret. Real smooth sippin', and wait 'til you taste the aftertaste!

Cup o' Culture: Tasty fluid civilization in a mug! The Planck-scale citizens of this particular culture are so small they live according to an extremely accelerated rate of time. Watch entire liquid civilizations rise and fall in a matter of seconds! The challenge of this potentially interactive brew is to hurry

---

[20] And Quing, alas, had neglected to splurge for the extended warranty/monkey-back guarantee.

up and chug it before it develops rocket technology and launches, thereby blowing off your head as you raise the mug to take a drink!

<u>Dehydrated Water</u>: The ultimate low calorie drink! Just add water and stir: *Instant water*! Goes great with The Space Between Food.

C'MON BY ON WEDNESDAY NIGHTS FOR OUR
BATTERED FISH SUPPORT GROUP!

Enjoy a pipin' hot bowl of Quing's special recipe *Primordial Soup* today! Free croutons grudgingly dispensed upon request.

THE GOSPEL OF QUXXXZXXX

Herewith explicating the dawn of life in the universe

1   Biscuit is the Way, the Tao of the All in Each. Biscuit is the all-encompassing beacon of light at the end of the tunnel of an otherwise drab, meaningless existence. Biscuit is the foundation stone, the building block of the limitless light of all that we will ever experience and never experience.

2   Biscuit is.
Biscuit was.
Biscuit will be.
Biscuit is you.
Biscuit is me.
Biscuit is us.
Biscuit is everything.
Biscuit is eternal.
Biscuit is infinite.
And vice versa.

3   Such was I told by God-Biscuit, and I believe Hir, because S/He hath said, *Have faith in Me or else.*

4   "Avoideth ye a lucky duck named Buck wearing mukluks and causing a ruckus in a woodchuck's truck, for he is a schmuck!" saith the God-Biscuit.

5   And with you, my humble chordate companion, I share this blessed wisdom.

6   Upon waking look thou to the west, toward the nefarious constellation of *Busty Lobster's Lament.* Backlit by the first rays of dawn, perform thee the Meditations of the Chimp Chomp. Place your freshly-chomped, newly-gimped and no doubt still-simpering chimp atop a no-skimp pimped-out shrimpin' blimp for the pimpled Gipper. Insert thee a pine cone into that belly-button that is thine as you ponder the sound of one hand clapping, consider thee the whereabouts of your fist after you open your hand, and weep thee for the plight of a hairball gone bald.

7 As you finish these meditations, turn thou to the east and behold the beauty of the rising sun. Yodel and/or bellow ye this hymn as loudly as possible:

The Battle Hymn of the God-Biscuit
Mine eyes have seen the glory of the rising of the Dough
S/He has banished the SpapOopGannopOlop who is Hir mighty foe,
S/He hath loosed the mighty Platypus whom we love and know
Hir Dough doth rise above!
Glory glory hallelujah! Hir Dough doth rise above!

I have denied my femur 'cause a pickle told me to
There's a tree sloth with no eyelids, just be glad it isn't you
I would tell you that I'm lying but that would not be true
Hir Yeast doth rise above!
Glory glory hallelujah! Hir Yeast doth rise above!

We, Hir chosen children, have Hir love ever to keep
God-Biscuit gives us spiffy things that come heap after heap
But when S/He mentions pineapple the angels they do weep
Hir Dough doth rise above!
Glory glory hallelujah! Hir Dough doth rise above!

8 If you perform this ritual faithfully every morning at the first light of morn, yodeling and/or bellowing the hymn at neighbor-wakening decibel levels, God-Biscuit will bless your soul/spleen.[21]

---

[21] Please refer to 'Appendix IV: The Nature of Bodily & Spiritual Existence' for additional information about the 'soul' and spleen.

9   So sayeth I who am Quxxxzxxx.

10   As I pen these immortal words, my agent insists I add the following clause: I wish to state that the opinions expressed herein are the views of myself and are likely biased by occurrences that have shaped my present belief system and are not necessarily the views or opinions or legally binding statements of me and/or I, and the following statements are not to be construed as endorsements of this, that or the other and vice versa, in perpetuity. I admit neither liability nor culpability for the actions of me, myself and/or neither/nor I.

11   Now that that's cleared up, let us continue: Shortly after defeating the vile SpapOopGannopOlop, God-Biscuit underwent a spiritual crisis and became an atheist. A strange universe it was in those days, when God was an atheist. So severe was Hir self-doubt, ennui and identity crisis that for a brief period S/He changed Hir name to **The Divinity Formerly Known as God-Biscuit**; finding that name to be insufficiently alliterative, S/He changed it to **Cooter Achilles Jr. the First**. That name failed to signify and, in a shameless attempt to pander to the lucrative gnostic-hip-hop youth demographic, S/He changed then to **DJ Demiurgus**; that name failed to catch on so, too lachrymose to care anymore, S/He gave up and reverted to being called God-Biscuit, much to everyone's relief.

12   Other times S/He would pull a *deus absconditus*, dispensing with the **Blessed Biscuitoid Bling-Bling**, firing Hir haberdasher and disappearing into the pleroma for aeons at a time. S/He disappeared for long periods with no explanation beyond a sign hung on a local neutron star that said, "Gone fission." Other times, however, God-Biscuit took on a physical body and argued with members of the Doughy Hosts over whether or not S/He existed.

13   When I pointed out that the mere fact that S/He could wonder whether or not S/He existed was proof *ipso facto* that S/He existed, God-Biscuit became mighty miffed and accused me of being an irascible and non-existent figment of Hir non-existent imagination, trying to fool Hir non-existent Self with explanations that were irrelevant because they (and S/He) did not exist.

14   During one of these debates a wise member of the Hosts named J'on'lillee convinced God-Biscuit that because S/He was basically All Things (what with being the Supreme Being and all), that not only did S/He not exist, S/He also did exist and was thus simultaneously a hardcore atheist and a devout worshipper of Hirself.

15   "God-Biscuit is in essence a manifestly non-existent and solipsistically-extroverted devoutly atheistic worshipper of Hirself," said J'on'lillee. "Those are the kinds of job expectations you have to deal with when you're Everything."

16   Everyone present concurred with such logic so, relieved, we dropped the matter like unto a flaming tuber.

17   Things were quiet thereafter until one day an Angelic Universal Scouting Party reported the discovery that life was developing naturally in the universe! And lo!, there was much rejoicing, exultation, and hootin' 'n hollerin'.

18   The first life forms we noticed were a small tribe of vaguely Sierpinski gasket-shaped organisms that had evolved on a remote planet called Tavist-D. Gentle they were, their voices a merry singsong chirp resulting from the helium-rich atmosphere of their home. They spoke in perfectly formed poetic couplets and sang simple melodies that enthused reverently about the beauty of the universe around them.

19   Alas, this gracefully noble and poetic species had the misfortune to have evolved body markings that perfectly mimicked the cosmosexual mod-inflected *Vera Wang* ensemble God-Biscuit was wearing when S/He arrived at the 'Dough a Go-Go/Welcome to Reality' party thrown at *Cipriani* on their behalf. Enraged that, not just one or two, but *the entire species* had come to the party in the exact same outfit as Hirs, S/He smote them all where they stood. The entire genome went instantaneously extinct, vaporized in a puff of helium and half-eaten finger sandwiches before any of us had time to alert God-Biscuit to the misunderstanding.

20   The next life form to catch our notice was named **Oozumgreep**, which is ancient Aramaic for "something-that-isn't-really-anything, but is sort of a little bit like a slimy mucus-flavored space turnip vacuum-sealed inside itself, (kind of)," which was nearly almost but not quite precisely

what it was: Primordial ooze with a gag reflex, undulating aimlessly, gurgling, and trying to digest slow-moving objects.
21   Raised in a dank and methane-rich atmosphere, the Oozumgreep was a smelly, useless and difficult-to-appreciate species. Within a few millennia it became painfully apparent that it was rapidly evolving into something else; what it would be we could not yet tell, though whatever it was involved propellers and an unconscionable amount of rayon.

**A Biscuitist Mandala: Meditate upon this symbol as
you flex your spleen while yodeling and/or bellowing
your praise to the God-Biscuit**

22   All of this time life had been sprouting up in other parts of the universe too. One common factor among life was that it eventually died.
23   Everything in our universe is composed of the flesh of God-Biscuit and contains Hir seed. Once the Divine Doughish seed is properly kneaded and baked it becomes what some call a *soul*, and is everlasting except that it has no form once its host body dies.

24   We were thus posed with a problem: what to do with all of the lost, wandering energy fields that made their way to Angelopolis after their bodies withered to dust? They overcrowded our movie theaters, antagonized our beloved pet quadrupeds and, being bodiless, were tax-exempt freeloaders.

25   For the solution, let us backtrack a bit: Far back, in the early days of the universe, God-Biscuit had mailed each member of the Doughy Hosts a brochure outlining the career choices open to each individual, along with any relevant information for those seeking to go into middle management, tips on unionizing for the Doughy Proletariat, &c.

26   One career option was that of zookeeper, which was chosen by an angel named Xanax. However, this was before any non-angelic life forms had evolved, so there were no animals to put into his zoo. He and his descendants eventually gave up in boredom and took up ping-pong.[22]

27   Over the aeons, Xanax had begat Fosamax, Fosamax begat Mucinex, Mucinex begat FedEx, FedEx begat Nasonex, Nasonex begat Crisco, Crisco begat Drano, Drano begat Leon, Leon begat Buck, Buck begat Chuck, Chuck begat Toilet Duck, Toilet Duck begat Goom, Goom begat Googam, Googam begat Groot, Groot begat Gonad, Gonad begat Ward, and Ward begat Jerry Mathers, as the Beaver.

28   Beaver, son of Ward and proud scion of the Xanax family heritage, was elated at the emergence of life, even something so inherently ambiguous, useless and repulsive as the Oozumgreep, for now his inherited legacy had a purpose: He would be zookeeper for the ultimate zoo, **Arglebargle the AbodeBiscuit**, where are warehoused the disembodied souls of the life forms of the universe.

29   God-Biscuit had decreed that upon death a soul's destiny would be determined by moral judgment of the life it had just finished. After payment of any outstanding rental fees (prorated according to how long the entity's *life span/lease option* had been, and based on how fashionable a planet the entity in question had inhabited) the soul would be transported to the afterlife it had earned.

---

[22] Please refer to footnote 88.

30   Good souls go to the *Golden Top of the Biscuit*, oft-called **Heaven**, where are situated the bountiful and beautiful Golden Fields of Earwax. There, in paradise, the blessed Biscuiteers are subject to festively drastic and joyously arbitrary experiments in post-death social engineering.

31   Bad souls go to the *Burnt Bottom of the Biscuit*, oft times called **Hell**, for as ye mix so shall ye bake. There, sinners atone for their transgressions by laboring forevermore in the loathsome Lint Mills of Arglebargle, emptying ashtrays in the bingo parlors of Angelopolis, or even worse, dredging the cesspools betwixt the ziggurats and geodesic domes of Quzzzxzzz's pre-owned chariot dealership.

32   *Truly* nasty souls are banished from this universe altogether, sentenced to a brutish, Hobbesian existence in **SpapOopGannopOlopOlis**, the wretched universe of the SpapOopGannopOlop, where a terrible time is had by all. This fate, which is far too awful to describe, is usually reserved only for *really* nasty life forms, but you never can tell because like all deities God-Biscuit is mighty, righteous, and quite arbitrary: Depending on the vicissitudes of reality at any given moment, just as God-Biscuit loves you, S/He also hates you (albeit in a friendly, nurturing way).

33   And so it doth be.

34   Aeons later, after life in the universe had become rather common, two members of the Doughy Hosts, named **Ph'on'zee** and **Sisyphus**, were pushing rocks around the rolling hills of an area that would one day be called by its inhabitants *Nutley, New Jersey*. Sisyphus, unfortunately so-named due to his debilitatingly severe lisp, was an alternately claustrophobic and agoraphobic mountain ranger. Feeling both confined and exposed, he was in a foul mood because his boulder kept rolling over his toe, so he decided to leave.

35   "Thith thuckth dude... thethe rockth keep thquithin' my toeth! By God-Bithcuit, thith ith pithin' me off! Thee ya later, Ph'on'thee," saith Sisyphus.

36   "Oculus-doculus,"[23] said Ph'on'zee. Waving goodbye to his friend, Ph'on'zee spent an invigorating afternoon

---

[23] "Oculus-doculus" = Latin for "Okey-dokey."

aerobicizing to the song *4'33"* by John Cage[24] and struggling to solve his all-white Zen Rubik's Cube. He had decided to leave when he came upon a colorless orange box of rain wearing a coonskin cap in a pigpen. The box was actively doing nothing and was doing so quite effectively.

37   Ph'on'zee stepped closer to examine the raining box when there was a vivid eidetic flash. Clearing his eyes he saw what looked to the untrained observer like a self-masticating unicorndog with a vigorously-steaming gullet.

38   From its gaping gullet the unicorndog, heavily hovering weightlessly and clearly enunciating the words sideways, asked Ph'on'zee:

39   "Have you ever seen me before?"

40   "No," answered Ph'on'zee.

41   "Then how do you know it's *me*?" the unicorndog demanded, festively twisting around into a Möbius Strip-Ouroboros shape and feeding itself to itself intravenously.

42   Ph'on'zee pondered the intricacies of the question, but before he could answer the unicorndog reversed its polarities. As a wave of metamorphosis rippled along the topological manifold of the unicorndog's body architecture it asked, "If I were me, what would I be doing right now?"

43   "You would be asking me questions, because you *are* you!" said Ph'on'zee, as the unicorndog undulated happily.

44   Giddy with mirth and reeling from overexposure to the malodorous reek of boiled and batter-dipped unicorn meat, Ph'on'zee lurched back. His foot hit a small rock and he fell into a puddle directly behind him. Embarrassed, he got up and spit into the puddle; the chance mixture of mud, amino acids, angel spit, and whatever else was in the puddle lay there gurgling and belching in the briny depths. Just then a lightning bolt struck, a meteorite splashed down for good measure, and a ratty old tire at the bottom of the puddle dissolved; thus was life created on Earth.

45   Neither Ph'on'zee nor the unicorndog were interested; they ignored it, thinking it to be just another obnoxious puddle. They spent the evening trying to figure

---

[24] The happening new fitness craze known as *aleatory aerobics*.

out why the word "dictionary" is included in the dictionary, and soon went their respective ways.

46   Within a few millennia the first life forms evolved on Earth, these being a tribe of walking pickles who were really quite racist.

Ph'on'zee, creator of life on Earth, showing off his all-white Zen Rubik's Cube in prehistoric Nutley, NJ

47   As one might imagine, nothing much happened during the reign of pickles as dominant life form on Earth, except when **That Meatball Which Creepeth** showed up. The walking pickles were gathered on their Neoproterozoic beach debating whether "inny" belly buttons are genetically superior to "outty" belly buttons, and if so whether eugenics programs were called for. All of a sudden That Meatball Which Creepeth came creeping over the horizon.

48   The walking pickles made a sound like unto gargling the goo from inside a lava lamp, which was the sound that walking pickles made when they were surprised.

49   That Meatball Which Creepeth, who is verily *THE Meatball Whom Doth Creep*, messily extracted from itself a smaller meatball, which had been nested inside like a Russian doll. Consisting of putrescent unicorn meat left over from a few paragraphs back, the mini-meatball just lay there, inert. Stitched into the meatball's anterior convex surface was a burgundy-colored monogram, a wine dark *C*, for behold, Charlie was its name.

50   That Meatball Which Creepeth said: "Behold! I bringeth forth unto ye Charlie, that meatball that is the utterly supreme meatball, the prototype meatball that shall be the forebear of our glorious new race! No mere Biscuit, this! Verily 'tis a meatball with which to reckon! None shall dare question this meatball, for 'tis the essence of purity and 'pon this meatball lie the seeds of our future! Yea, about this meatball our descendents will sing songs of exultation for generations undreamt!"

51   That Meatball Which Creepeth looked around, expecting the crowds to go wild with approval. Instead, the pickles merely looked puzzled.[25]

52   The meatball equivalent of a blush rippled across the meatball equivalent of That Meatball Which Creepeth's face, and That Meatball Which Creepeth consulted its intergalactic translation dictionary. Instead of the rousing speech intended, in the walking pickles' rudimentary click language it translated into, "10-4 good buddy: Monkey Pfister is happy even though we are infested with flies that have steaks instead of eyes."

53   No wonder the pickles looked confused; realizing it had taken a wrong turn after leaving the *Motel 6* at Alpha Centauri, That Meatball Which Creepeth quickly crept off into the sunset and was never again seen on Earth.

---

[25] As puzzled as one could reasonably expect, that is, considering the severely limited emotional and expressive range of a prehistoric self-motile pickle.

54   The walking pickles lasted only a few centuries; as there were no other life forms on the planet against whom to be racist, they eventually hated themselves into extinction in a vinegary and genocidal *gherkins vs. dills* civil war.

55   The next major life forms were the dinosaurs, a thunder lizard empire that ruled the Earth for tens of millions of years. The dinosaurs' name for themselves was *SATOR AREPO TENET OPERA ROTAS*, which translates into contemporary English as, "We have disproportionately short arms but manage to impress the ladies nevertheless."

56   Like "SATOR AREPO TENET OPERA ROTAS," all names, words, and even the grammatical and syntactical structures of the dinosaurian language were palindromes, because dinosaurs were quite severely dyslexic. Dinosaur semioticians reasoned that if a word is spelled the same way backwards and forwards it doesn't matter whether one accidentally reads it in reverse, so they designed their language with an accordingly high level of palindromically-reversible information entropy.[26] Prone to typing in all-caps due to the blunt stubbiness of their digits, their name for God-Biscuit was *QAOXOMOXOAQ*, and their name for Earth was, unfortunately, *POOP*, which, alas, is a palindrome too.

57   Having grown decadent from two hundred million years of obsessing over analytic cubism, *mille-feuille*, and pornographic haiku about Kermit the Frog[27], the dinosaurs eventually succumbed to environmental catastrophe.

58   Most of the power resources of present-day planet Earth exist in the form of fossilized and/or liquefied dinosaur remains. This necessarily posed a problem to the dinosaurs

---

[26] *Exempli gratia,*

$$H(S) = -\sum_i p_i \sum_j p_i(j) \sum_k p_{i,j}(k) \ \log \ p_{i,j}(k).$$

[27] Such as the following:

> Green, and full of need
> hot amphibious lover
> spanks piggy's plump rump.

or:

> Wart-covered frog
> moans, croaking in ecstasy
> gropes the willing pork.

themselves, who were in no hurry to fossilize and/or dissolve themselves into liquid form, so plentiful and affordable energy was always an issue for their empire.

59   Once the wheel was finally invented, privatized dinosaur energy conglomerates decided to generate power by exploiting the labor of the proletarian protomammal caste, forcing tiny hamster-like protomammals to run on hamster-wheels. This disastrous idea precipitated a worldwide extinction event,[28] leaving the dinosaurs no choice but to

---

[28] As explained by the BiscuiTemple's in-house energy economist, Señor Yngwië Hëinrich Plöpzalöt, Ph.D., the dinosaur-induced planetary extinction event was caused thusly:

"The average Cretaceous hamster-like protomammal in question (henceforth referred to in layman's terms as "hamster") weighed roughly two ounces and could run the equivalent of six feet per second, turning the hamster wheel roughly 5.15 revolutions per second. Attached to generators, it took 150 hamsters running nonstop to power a single light bulb in the typical middle class ranch-style duplex popular with dinosaurs during the late stages of their empire. Of course, no hamster can run 24 hours a day, so the total requirement to light an incandescent bulb over the course of a day was 3,600 hamsters working in shifts. Ergo, providing the power for a single dinosaur household required 475,000 hamsters a year, producing 7.1 kilowatts of power.

"Multiplying this number of hamsters by the number of dinosaur households in the late Cretaceous period yields a THR (Total Hamster Requirement) of +/- 11.94 trillion hamsters a year to meet energy demand. The sheer weight and impact of that many hamsters quickly took its toll on the planet's ecosphere, made worse by the shortened life span of such overworked hamsters, resulting in 2 billion tons of DHBPA (Depleted Hamster Biomass Per Annum).

"This problem was exacerbated by the enormous amount of food required to feed twelve trillion hard-working hamster-like protomammals. A typical hamster requires 15 grams of food per day, with the total worldwide hamster workforce requiring nearly 114 billion tons of food annually. The dinosaurs were forced to terraform nearby planets just to handle the increased demand for oats, wheat and other tasty carb-loaded munchies suitable for hard-working hamsters.

"In a decision with devastating consequences, comets were towed in from the distant reaches of the solar system to be melted

learn the art of Mass Astral Projection. They quickly left their ruined home planet to explore the farthest reaches of the cosmos, "To boldly go where no enormous astral-projecting dyslexic lizard has gone before," as the popular phrase goes.

60   After the dinosaurs came a strange species of creature called the hornulus, an imbecilic beast with a tail nearly four kilomillimeters in length. Hornuli famously secreted a fruity odor (like sauerkraut made with prunes instead of cabbage) that attracted large numbers of bugs, for which it was handy to have a long tail with which to swat at them. Unfortunately for the hornulus, there was a ginormous spike at the tip of this tail, on which it would inevitably impale itself and die.[29]

---

down for water, since the bulk of Earth's freshwater aquifers had long since been metabolically converted to hamster urine. Alas, dinosaurs notoriously had very stubby fingers and lacked opposable thumbs, and so never could tie knots very well; while one of these comets was being towed in from the Oort Cloud the loop knot came undone and the comet slipped free of the cargo hold, slamming into the planet, causing worldwide devastation and dooming the dinosaurs to bodily extinction."

[29] The only reason the hornulus has any historical relevance whatsoever is that it illustrates just how far from perfection the course of evolution can be; in fact, self-impaled hornulus fossils are often used as counterexamples in debates between evolutionary biologists and Intelligent Design creationists, neither side knowing precisely whether the example of the hornulus helps or hurts their respective argument.

61   Next came the era of the mythical creatures and the fairy tale animals. Their reign was a short one, however, as **The Great Porridge Famine** of 212,000 B.C. decimated the thriving population of minotaurs, fairies and talking bears. Destitute and forced at last to eat their own gingerbread-based architecture, their civilization disappeared without a trace when the last frog prince forlornly croaked his final croak.

62   A little farther down the evolutionary line a bizarre mating ritual between a monkey and an eggplant went horribly awry, producing the world's first upright-walking hominid: *Homo sapiens*, the human being.

What Happens in ArglebargleOpolis Stays In ArglebargleOpolis: When next you visit the Afterlife, enjoy the wonderfully counterintuitive architecture and neighborly hospitality of the *Storage Shed of Pre-Owned Souls*, conveniently located in the heart of the Arglebargle AbodeBiscuit warehouse district!

CANTO IV

THE APOCRYPHAL GOSPEL OF THE NUCLEAR PLATYPUS

Herewith illuminating the alchemical revelation of the Monotreme of Majesty

"Here the vulgar eye will see naught but obscurity and will despair considerably."

—Dr. John Dee
Monas Hieroglyphica, 1564

1   In My bib overalls and porkpie hat I stood beside My thresher, across the gully from yonder Golden Fields of Earwax. Much was happening and much was not happening, and vice versa. There appeared to appear above the sky a great tumult, and a swirling isobaric vortex appeared to appear above Me, ringed by an isometric drawing of an isochromatic isosceles hamburger.

2   In the days of 18 and 4 there appeared to appear within the vortex the image of the Glorious God-Biscuit Hirself, accompanied by Hir stunt double and wearing Marie Antoinette's personal *robe à la polonaise*, purchased for a premium price from auction at *Sotheby's*, with lederhosen and a gabardine suit from *Commes des Garçon*. S/He gazed in all directions simultaneously, for S/He is full of eyes roundabout.[30] Giving unto Me an air kiss S/He didst say, "Never have I been S/He who is that which is not the Absence of Nothing, and vice versa," and disappeared to where the rivers of Our vision flow into one another.

---

[30] And believe you Me, Hir monthly budget for custom-built sunglasses is accordingly massive.

3   And lo!, Quxxxzxxx and his brother Quzzzxzzz did come walking down the path. Stepping over a drainage canal they approached and asked Me whether I knew the time.

4   Ah, the time; I, who am truly He who is, had recently lost My pocket watch, so I licked My tongue and from within there was an inside-out ice cube whose parallel image was a leg with many arms that couldn't hear itself not speak, and the sound waves it didn't make while not speaking produced light rays of an amazing intensity, capable of penetrating nothing but themselves in a fashionable manner that made Me realize that never have things not been what they haven't otherwise appeared not to be as I sat down and walked beyond flat mountains overlooking wine dark seas of evaporated water, walking like a good night's sleep towards a place that was not there but perhaps one day would appear in forgotten accounts of future history, telling Me all the while in its droning, sonorous voice that if I were to lick a frog it would spell certain disaster, even if the frog offered to gargle with a meat cleaver thus allowing Me to roam among the hillsides while happily running in terror from imaginary predators, dribbling and itching terribly after a quick visit with the **ChronoClapClam**, a time-traveling Mollusk of Mayhem pustulently infested with every form of venereal disease in the history of the universe[31], inspiring Me to think no thoughts at all except perhaps of inverted horizons occupying a garden of immense dimensions in the realm of the outer fringes of time, to produce sounds never before seen by anyone as I gazed down upon the back of My head and the atmosphere momentarily became everything *except a fried egg that loves Me*, and then I noticed, spewing and spurting forth from the severed corpus callosum of an amphibious bat that's afraid of the dark and addicted to sunscreen (and trying to make the best of an unfortunate situation), a nocturnally-

---

[31] The theme song of ChronoClapClam's short-lived afternoon TV program, *Heavy Petting with C³*, began with the lines,
> "I love you, you love me,
> I just gave you herpes simplex 3,
> Just you try not to pick at the scabs,
> Oh by the way you now have crabs."

challenged flying rodent, a verifiably veritable verbal-vegetable opiate is this bat, this amphibious assault ventricle, alas not a crustacean with charisma but at the very least a chordate with class and a paragon of decrepitude that created its own spontaneously-retroactive birth defect, comrade to a vegetable with vim and vigor; of whom do I speak, why none other than the scaredy-bat's second cousin's step-uncle thrice-removed, **Sir Mohrdahk, Sea Cucumber With An Attitude**, née *Marvin Melvin* and his wife *Melvina Marvina* née *Doris Boris*, champion of stuff, of cognitive objects long lost within the minds of daring young men and women in the future, brave unborn people whose ideas are dormant within their brains just waiting to be inspired by the heroic actions of a lower-order organism barely evolved from a level of mud, a powerful inspiration able to vomit out its own innards and turn itself inside-out as a decoy for approaching enemies, with no actual cortex or any mental functions at all beyond the most rudimentary instinctual survival responses necessary for perpetuation of the most basic daily existence imaginable, plus remembrance of grudges and a chip looking for a shoulder on a creature without skeletal structure,[32] so I tried to ignore what I hadn't done but My attention span was too short to ignore anything and I forced Myself not to realize that I hadn't actually realized anything, yet I knew I must not abstain from denying abstinence because outside is a big

---

[32] However, I digress: the fried egg that loves Me was nicely contained as a crystallized thought standing astride itself as it trailed off to infinity, having out-of-body experiences directly behind My face and trying spontaneously not to decapitate Myself in a valiant attempt to bless Our friends and lovers for seeing, hearing and smelling purposes and above all a life-affirming event as I tried to fold the grapefruit of My childhood into a force to be reckoned with by anyone who would dare stand in the shadow of a severely intangible isopod wrapped in the gossamer threads of the *Erinyes* that was exactly like, except completely different from, trying to swallow a long-distance hippopotamus that could burp up entire school buses in a single shot and which had just proposed itself into existence with the ability to smell the colors of a single sound drifting gently in the wind.

place, indicating that this sentence is a lie, which may not be truthful because I am absolutely unsure of everything and I am indecisive even in My agnosticism,[33] and I have now forgotten how to forget things so I now remember everything, for yea and behold, I am the Nuclear Platypus ever and anon, and—

5   [—*gurgle*—]

6   Quzzzxzzz had just bespoiled My Proustian reverie, erasing My daydream with the type of gurgle that bodes ill.

7   Quxxxzxxx appeared most impatient, looking at Me and tapping his foot in the otolithic soil. His torso newly covered roundabout with tattoos of couches in all styles and price ranges, he repeated his question. "Do You know the time, please?"

8   "Yes," I answered, puffing on My corncob pipe, "The time is now-o'clock."

9   Satisfied, Quxxxzxxx and Quzzzxzzz turned and walked back down the path. I wiped the sweat from My brow with My flipper and scanned the horizon distractedly. 'Twas time to harvest the latest earwax bonanza.

"I come to you in the night with buckets of melted cheese."
—Quxxxzxxx & Quzzzxzzz,
Narcoleptic Dairy Enthusiasts Association Conference

---

[33] Though I'm not so sure about that.

That Dough of which we cannot bake, we must pass over in silence.

<u>A glimpse inside the mind of the Monotreme of Might</u>: He revs up His thresher, ready for a tough but fulfilling day of harvesting the Golden Fields of Earwax (located in Heaven just past the Piggly Wiggly on Interstate 16 [take a left at Metatron's Mini-Mart], beyond the south-western suburbs of Arglebargle the AbodeBiscuit).

An honest day of work for an honest and hard-workin' Platypus… oft-times that's all a Messiah-type feller wants.

CANTO V

THE GOSPEL OF QUZZZXZZZ

Herewith expounding upon the rise and fall and rise of human civilization on Earth

1   A major breakthrough in the history of every species is the discovery and taming of fire. In fact, alongside the creation of a written language, the discovery of fire is often *the* pivotal event in a species' development.[34]

2   So it was that four million years after the end of chapter three, when humanity had established itself as the dominant life form on Earth, second-rate actor and B-myth Greek godlet **Amateurmetheus** decided to assist the early humans by helping them skip all that messy business with fire and advance directly to the level of deep-fat fryers.

3   Hot-wiring a time-machine[35] from the tool shed of his cranky old neighbor Chronos, he took a few fryers back into the distant past, when humanity consisted of only five people: Nosaj Nala, Paralyza Minnelli, Potrzebie the Guru, Vern the RoadToad, and their faithful Neanderthal manservant, Olduvai George.[36]

4   Less accomplished than his step-uncle Prometheus, Amateurmetheus had forgotten that there were no power sources way back in the distant olden days of yore, so he and the other five set out to build a small power plant. Just as the power plant was finished a bizarre accident occurred, involving sparks from a Tesla coil and a puddle of olibanum

---

[34] Especially if the species in question suddenly discovers itself to be extremely and instantaneously flammable.

[35] A top-of-the-line *Antikytheran Chrononaut Doohickulus X-290*.

[36] Olduvai had a tendency to wander aimlessly, and was thus really more a *Meanderthal* than Neanderthal.

from Potrzebie's tipped-over pyxidium. Alas, all six of them were electrocuted, completely pre-empting the human race.[37]

5   Nosaj, Paralyza, Potrzebie and Vern went forth from the **Kitchen of Eden** and multiplied themselves happily, and in a short time the human race had festively infested every nook and cranny of the planet.

6   Early on, humanity was guided along the initial steps to self-determination by door-to-door intergalactic Space Squid missionaries, who implanted the dual concepts of religion and Biscuits into human minds.

7   The idea of a Biscuit as Supreme Being was popular and long served as a strong "roll" model for early humanity, making Biscuitism the One True Religion for many hundreds of thousands of years.

8   Early humanity was content to sit in trees and think about Biscuits, as was the custom in those days. Millennia later a bored wise guy, possibly an unwitting pawn of the SpapOopGannopOlop, jokingly proposed the idea of civilization and messed up everything.

9   Alas, civilization quickly took root and became *The Ultimate Quest For A Good Biscuit*, for the visits of the Space Squids had long since ceased.[38]

10   Now that humanity was on its own, nomadic tribes roamed the planet in search of wild untamed Biscuits, but these grew quite scarce after centuries of over-harvesting. Eventually the nomads settled down and created agriculture, hoping to find a way to grow Biscuits. This too proved futile.

---

[37] Because humanity went extinct prematurely Amateurmetheus was never born, so in all actuality this never happened. By causing the premature extinction of humanity, Amateurmetheus prevented *himself*, the very cause of humanity's extinction, from coming into being, thereby ensuring humanity's survival. It's dilemmas like this that keep most people from messing around with the timestream, and the dutiful reader is hereby warned against attempting such an idea him- or herself.

[38] The Space Squids' mighty galactic empire had collapsed after a questionable Shi'ar hedge fund debacle left most of them destitute, down and out bums on Squid Row.

11 Although early attempts to create Biscuits were doomed to failure, two good things happened as a result of the quest: Fire was finally tamed in an effort to advance baking technology, and the wheel was invented by proto-Biscuitist shamans, its round shape being soothing to frustrated humans, reminiscent as it is of a very large Biscuit.

12 Druidic Biscuit-worshippers gathered, gesticulating frantically at massive megalithic stone circles like Dough-Henge and Gobekli Tepe. Ere long, city-states like Çatal Hüyük and those in Egypt, Sumer, and Ninevah formed as the raging masses congregated in desperate attempts to locate someone who knew how to obtain a good Biscuit.

13 Most of these early city-states and agricultural communities spoke a common language called Proto-IndoBiscuitoidian, from which all modern languages are descended. This language had over 3,000 words for "Biscuit" alone, the most common of which was "sunne", or, more often, "sun." Alas, most historians do not bother translating this word when they report that nearly all of the ancient religions were sun cults, which is true except for the fact that the meaning of "sun" is misrepresented by these (possibly SpapOopGannopOlopOlist) establishment historians.

14 As attempts to harvest, grow or create Biscuits ended in dismal failure, people around the globe were despondent over the dearth of Dough. Self-induced plagues and wars ravaged the planet, mass hysteria reigned, and humanity was seemingly on the road to extinction, oblivion-bound in the fast lane.

15 "My God-Biscuit, my God-Biscuit, why hast thou forsaken us?!?" wailed the masses of humanity, wallowing in lugubriousness. Troubadours and minstrels raised their voices to the heavens with songs of lamentation, having fallen into the pits of Doughlessness and despair.

16 In 4200 B.C.[39] a great prophet named Corncobbus founded **The Fellowship of the Fraternitatis of the Consecration of the Cathedral of the Veneration of the Sanctification of the Abbey of the Sanctuary of the Chapel**

---

[39] B.C. = **B**efore **C**rustiness

of the Congregation of the Tabernacle of the Order of the Lodge of the Order of the Tabernacle of the Congregation of the Chapel of the Sanctuary of the Abbey of the Sanctification of the Veneration of the Cathedral of the Consecration of the Fraternitatis of the Fellowship of the First BiscuiTemple of the Nuclear Platypus Church of Arglebargle, Biscuitoidian Platypoid Orthodox, the propagators of the *Arglebarglian Biscuitist Society* upon the planet Earth. Since that fateful day over 6,000 years ago, the Church of Arglebargle has been *the* major force in the shaping of human experience, the global authority upon which the infrastructure of world history has been built.

Accept no imitations: Founded in 4200 B.C. by Pope Corncobbus the First, only the Nuclear Platypus Church of Arglebargle can truthfully claim to be *The World's Oldest and Largest Biscuit Cult.*

17   It was **Pope Corncobbus the First** who helped rally humanity under the banners of happiness once again, preaching the mystical doctrines of old-fashioned Orthodox Biscuitism that had been revealed unto him in a flash while on the road to Doughmascus. Pope Corncobbus was a great man who knew that glorious things were coming.

18   Ere long Corncobbus was proven right, for in **The First Coming** the Nuclear Platypus mated with the energies of the God-Biscuit Hirself and manifested Himself in the body of a woman (an event referred to by Doughist theologians as **The Immaculate Self-Boinkage**). Thus on midsummer morn was born unto Herself the venerable and wise prophet **Ped Xing**.[40] And, lo!, the Divine Dough was put forth in the body of a mortal, come to Earth to save humanity from a dystopian, Biscuitless future.

19 Verily forsooth, Ped Xing was infused with *The Flour Power of the Divine Dough*, for Her radiant soul had been freshly baked to perfection within *The Great White Light of the Oven on High*. She traveled across all of the world astride Her faithful pig **Hamulus**, enlightening the masses with the glorious message of the God-Biscuit. Even today Her impact is felt, as evidenced by the many "Ped Xing" signs that mark trails whithersoever She once traveled.

20 Ped and Her disciples, known as Pedheads, sailed the seven seas in a gravy boat called **Dougha's Ark**. They journeyed even unto the Americas, where, dressed in Her finest faux-Bigfoot-fur overcoat, Ped spread the message of the Doughist gospel among the tribal centers and early civilizations of the New World.[41]

21 In Her most itinerant phase Ped traveled extensively across Tibet, resplendent in Her radiance; in legend She is renowned as the blessed and venerable **Dalai Parton**.

22 Two of Ped's favored acolytes were the humble Doughist pilgrims *Hao Yu Doon*, son of Jah Neebee Guüd and Peggy Tsu, and *Al Denté*, firstborn of Anna Nigma and Adam Zapple. These two fine men were Robin Hood types, antiauthoritarians working to bring justice to the downtrodden, to enlighten the Neolithic lumpen proletariat with the White Light of the Divine Dough. Eventually the two rabble-rousers were imprisoned in the remote Punjabi fiefdom of the Itchy Twitcher, where they were assassinated by being forced to think of cheeseplugs and to view invisible corn.

---

[40] Thereby completing the *Holy Trinity*: God-Biscuit, the Nuclear Platypus and Ped Xing. The Trinity is truly **The Divine Triscuit**.

[41] In a case of severe linguistic drift across the millennia, thousands of years later in the holy temples of *Itza Chikken*, Mexico, the Mayans became obsessed with human sacrifice when an errant translation of the Biscuitist Codex led them to believe that human blood made an excellent gravy component of Biscuits 'n gravy.

23   In homage to these fine men, Ped Xing wrote Her most beloved poem, *The Lament of Ped Xing*. This Doughist Dirge was lost for millennia until rediscovered in 1379 A.D.[42] at a garage sale in Canterbury by Geoffrey Chaucer, who translated it from Ped's original Proto-IndoBiscuitoidian cuneiform manuscript into 14th-century Middle English:[43]

The Lament of Ped Xing
(Translation copyright © 1379 by Geoffrey Chaucer)

Juyste the gowde oul' boyes
neuver meenyng noe hearm
Beetes eall yow evre sawhe
been inne trowbel wyth the lauwe
Synnes the daie thei was borun.

Streyghtenyn' the cyrves
Flattynyng the hylls
Soumedaye the mountayne myghte gyte theime
Bot the lauwe neuver wille.
Mayckyn' thayre weie
the onely weie theiy knaue howhe
Thate's juyste a lytylle bytte moare
than the lauwe wille aloue

Juyste the gowde oul' boyes
wouoldn't chaynge if thei could
Fiyteyn' the sistem
liycke a treuwe moderne daie Robeyn Hwde.

Yeeeee-Haw!!

---

[42] A.D. = **A**fter **D**oughiness

[43] Chaucer's version, originally written in anapestic pentameter, was in turn translated by Waylon Jennings into contemporary vernacular English for use as the theme song for *The Dukes of Hazzard* television show in 1979, the 600th anniversary of Chaucer's authoritative translation. So, although this *looks* like a translation of the Dukes of Hazzard theme song into Chaucerian Middle English, rest assured that it is actually the other way around.

24   Ped eventually returned to the Mongol tribes into which She had been born, where She wrote down the Biscuitist philosophies and gospels that later missionaries compiled into **The Nuclear Platypus Biscuit Bible**. With this project finally underway, Ped set out to save humanity from Doughlessness. The crucial factor in humanity's salvation was that a good recipe for Biscuits finally be revealed, with the finished product to be dispensed unto the masses through a worldwide network of Church bake sales.

25   Unfortunately, tragedy struck before the logistics and planning for the bake sales were finalized. After Her widely publicized pay-per-view sermon known as *The Salmon on the Mount*, word got out that Ped and the Mongol tribes knew how to make good Biscuits, resulting in the mass human migrations known colloquially by historians as *The Great Biscuit Crusades*. The Biscuiteers erected the Great Wall of China to fend off the uncivilized hordes of Biscuit-

mongers, crazed barbarians driven beyond sanity by life-long denial of Dough and by their lustful need of a Biscuit.

26   Eventually the fanatical hordes of Dough-cravers broke through the Biscuiteers' defenses, and in the chaos Ped slipped on a puddle of *Pam No-Stick Cooking Spray* and fell into the huge baking ovens. As She died Her soul rose to the heavens, opening up like unto a Biscuit awaiting a smear of margarine at the first light of dawn. Her mourners wailed and wept, crying, "Behold! She is risen and ready for baking!"

27   In the wake of this tragic event it was prophesied that, because Ped Xing had baked for the common good, the Dough would rise again.

28   The only solace left to the Biscuitoid masses was this touching ode to grace, written in alliterative verse by Pope

Corncobbus himself in homage to his lost friend and inspiration:

Ode to Ped Xing
Here's the story of a lovely lady
Most blessed by the Deity of Dough
God-Biscuit's chosen one, Her Dough is risen
With a crusty golden glow

Here's the story of a Nuclear Platypus
Who was dealing with problems of His own
Like smiting the God-Biscuit's unbelievers
For their sins they must atone

'Til the one day when She met this Quasi-Mammal
And they knew it was much more than a fling
That these two could bake the new Messiah
That's the way they fused and turned into Ped Xing

Into Ped Xing, into Ped Xing,
That's the way that they fused into Ped Xing

29 In the meantime, however, prospects did not look good. With the Earthly form of the Biscuitist Messiah now baked beyond recognition, the Church of Arglebargle was suddenly a non-prophet organization. Even worse, the only written Biscuit recipe had gone up in flames along with Ped.

30 A cadre of high-ranking Pedheads tried to remember the recipe, and a few actually attempted to bake from scratch. It is from these valiant yet ill-fated attempts that we get what passes for a Biscuit these days. Modern "biscuits" are mere echoes of the True Glory of an Old-Fashioned, Biblically-Proportioned Biscuit. A "biscuit" today is like a shadow on the wall of Plato's Cave, flickering invitingly but in truth distracting the earnest yeast-seeker from the glories that await if only the eyes could pierce the veils of illusion and Dough Deprivation.

31 Alas, the feeble imitation "biscuits" were not enough. With the loss of Ped Xing and the only written Biscuit recipe, the Church and humanity as a whole did not fare well. Civilization plunged into chaos, throwing humanity back into the Stone Age and taking with it nearly all historical records of the events just described.[44]

32   It is rumored that Pope Corncobbus died in 3615 B.C. at the age of 603, when a rampaging posse of mixed metaphors attacked him in a rain forest. Like a wolf in sheep's clothing on its last legs, Corncobbus was savaged as it rained cats and dogs until the cows came home, like a fox in a henhouse when the chickens at last come home to roost.

33   His successor to the Papal throne, Pope Beendippicus of Cnossos, mandated in a series of decretals that the only way to bring humanity back from the brink of savagery was to reunite them under the banners of Biscuitism. Covert agents trained in the Doughist Doctrines went forth into the world to plant the seeds of Biscuitism in the minds of eager new generations of humanity, for whom the Glorious Biscuitist Empires of old had become little more than nostalgic legend and myth. Bizarre, secretive men and women approached fledgling empires and dynasties, offering valuable advice in exchange for a position in the royal court; invariably what would begin as a servile position would change dramatically as Biscuitist agents became the shadowy source of power behind the throne.

34   Earlier, during the glory days of Ped Xing's work, the Biscuiteers had invented paper for wrapping Biscuits sold and

---

[44] The 1970s television show *Alice* was originally to be a sitcom about the zany exploits of the doomed *Operation: Biscuit Recipe Reclamation/Resurrection* team. Mel's Diner was to be the classified Tibetan research facility of a coalition of Neolithic Biscuitoid Mutants and stranded Space Squid hangers-on attempting to recreate Ped's Biscuit recipe from scratch. The show was to be called **ALIS**, for **A**ctive **L**iving **I**ntelligence **S**ystem, about the introgression of the Divine Dough plasmate into the fabric of human consciousness via an occult technique called PKD, for Psycho-Kinetic Doughism. The waitress Flo's catch-phrase of "Kiss my grits!" was to have been "Knead my Dough!", playing on the homophonic punnery of 'knead' and 'need', reminding viewers of how much they need/knead to accept God-Biscuit into their hearts, or at least their stomachs. Alas, after making the rounds of script doctors and bean-counters the resulting show as broadcast bore little resemblance to the original lofty premise.

bartered from the drive-thru Biscuit stands along the old Silk Road. Alas, due to the collapse of civilization there were no more roadside Biscuit stands, and so writing was invented so all those surplus Biscuit wrappers could at least be used for *something*. With this new use for paper the message of Doughism would spread far and wide.

Ped Xing baked to justify your sins: Shown here in Her blessed guise of the Dalai Parton, rallying the Biscuitist faithful to the Doughist cause outside the main *BiscuiTemple Lodge & Bingo Parlor* in Biscuitropolis, Tibet, shortly before Her tragic death.

35 Rev. Speemophilocles the Aborborygmatous was the chief adviser to seven generations of the Erqmopklma Sasquatchi Dynasty during the period 3200-2700 B.C. With his devoted pet Pootie the Half-Lizard/Half-Doughnut, he used the Biscuit wrappers to write one of the earliest known books, called *Würlde Withoute Scabs. Würlde Withoute Scabs* remains one of the most philosophically profound works of all time, as can be seen in this excerpt from page 140:

> Thee Godd-Byscuit is onne of manny and the Firstt amung Them; though S/He is noww All Theengs, at firstt S/He was onnly Onne. In Hir arre thee four ellemments yett S/He is and is nott an ellemment. S/He is a spirrit yett has a univerrsil boddy. S/He is and is nott an isosceles hammburrger and yet S/He is and is nott a

cheeeseplugg. S/He was thee Firstt and S/He shall be thee Last. And vice verrsa and nonne of thee abovve.

There is no Godd but Byscuit and S/He is the Godd-Byscuit. There is no Byscuit but Godd and S/He is the Byscuit-Godd. There is no Godd-Byscuit but Godd-Byscuit and S/He is the Godd-Byscuit.

36 Rev. Speemophilocles' magnum opus is significant not only because it is the ur-text from which the English language arose, it also introduced one of the most widely-loved words ever spoken in human language, the word "aborborygmatous," meaning *to do something in a smelly manner*. Equally important, the book contains the first known mention of the Ritual of the Dehydrated Watermelon, an idea synonymous with stark terror in the race memory of nearly every culture on the planet. Most crucial, however, was the role *Würlde Withoute Scabs* played in the spread of Doughism far and wide.

37 As *Würlde Withoute Scabs* topped the best-seller lists, it wasn't long before the governments of nearly every society on Earth, from the western-most borders of Europe and Africa and the desolate, high plains of Asia, to the island continent of Lemuria, the Native American cultures in the New World and the Antarctic Sasquatchi Empire, were once again under the control of the Doughist Papacy.

38 By this point the Church of Arglebargle was on the verge of once more publicly declaring its existence, as it was powerful enough to withstand outside threats. Unfortunately, the new problems that arose started within the highest echelons of the Church itself. The calamitous results of the actions performed by these renegade inner factions would reverberate down the halls of history for time immemorial.

39 The first concrete proof of a conspiracy dates from 617 B.C., when Pope Poioq the Plaid, advocate of a harsh schismatic strain of Fundamentalist Biscuitism called **The Rolling Pin of Wrath**, was assassinated. Unknown assailants fooled Poioq into eating far more potato salad than any human body could ever realistically hope to digest and metabolize in a single sitting. Because of the deviousness of this assault it is safe to assume that it was the result of years of calculated planning and effort.

40 In another instance, renegade forces gained access to the bingo parlors of the Hooterville BiscuiTemple and coated all of the corridors with a mixture of melted chicken fat and vinegar, creating a greasy mess that generated a foul odor not unlike the smell of a lard-dipped Broiled Boll Weevil Brisket.

An archaeologist's rubbing of Sasquatchi hieroglyphics, believed to depict a spiky and unpleasant "Cosmic Pineapple" involved in *The Unspeakably Gruesome Pineapple Insertion/Ingestion Incident*

41 Incidents of this sort happened for years until the renegade group felt it had gained enough power to emerge into open existence. So it was that in the year 523 B.C. the pro-SpapOopGannopOlopian organization, **The League In Support of Clam Enemas**, began operating in public. While originally passing itself off as an avant-garde conceptual lepidopterist knitting team for the upcoming Olympic games in Athens, it soon became obvious that something was amiss.

42 Enraged to have fallen for the then-new *Have you got any Grey Poupon?* joke, the Greek philosophers **Mediocrates the Dull** and **Testikles the Delicate**, with Roman General **Sporkus Maximus,** had founded the League with the goal of total domination, the creation of a worldwide surveillance-state empire to be ruled by the authoritarian nightmare known as **Santa Claus**.[45] This global police state, with the yearning masses of humankind crushed beneath the bespangled, curly-toed jackboots of **Billy Carter** and his fierce master race of Teutonic elf stormtroopers, would be the final prerequisite for the return of the SpapOopGannopOlop to our reality.

43   Coups became commonplace as the Arglebarglists and Clam Enemites incapacitated one another, leaving entire governments foundering as the secret power bases collapsed. The only group to benefit during this period, which lasted from 515 B.C. to 244 B.C., were the potato salad manufacturers, who became the world's first multinational conglomerates due to their products' astounding (if unlikely) popularity as the weapon of choice for political assassination.

44   The Clam Enemites used their arcane skills to put a curse on the Biscuitist Papacy, causing fifteen Popes in a row to accidentally hang and/or decapitate themselves during gruesome incidents of F.W.I.[46]

45   Herewith is presented a list of those thus victimized:
- Pope "Tater" McGee 20.4[nd] the Pustulent
- Pope Snarky the Flatulent, the VIIst
- Buford G. Jordan the 0th, the Pimped-Out Pope
- Quasimodo and Quasimoda, the Coed Popes
- Cletus the 5st, the Podunk Pope
- Pope Epop, the Palindromic Pope
- Pope Myron "Mango" Bartholomew the 23th
- John Q. Public, the Populist Pope
- Pope Gorski the 7rd, Paragon of Exemplartude
- Prunella III.14, the Pi Pope
- Pope Junior Sr., Jr., the Redundant Pope
- Nerdley & Lardella McNerdley, the Elopin' Popes
- Pope "Tootie" Biff, aka Gomer McGomez the 3nd

46   Shortly thereafter the League stepped up its attacks considerably. One of the most effective tactics was to sponsor

---

[45] e.g., "He's making a list, checking it twice, gonna find out who's naughty or nice," and, "He sees you when you're sleeping, he knows when you're awake, he knows if you've been bad or good so be good for goodness sake," &c.

[46] F.W.I. = **F**lossing **W**hile **I**ntoxicated

contests to find out who could create the best parody of Biscuitism. These parodic joke religions were presented as actual belief-systems and are the basis of today's religious institutions. This was a very effective way to sabotage the Church of Arglebargle's power: By flocking to these other religions the yearning masses were swayed from the Path of Biscuiteousness, for they knew not that one has but to look inside oneself to find the True Biscuit, for the True Biscuit is an integral part of all life in the universe.

47 [47]

48 The situation of the Church took a drastic turn for the worse in 321 A.D. when, under mysterious circumstances, the voluminous **Pope Spittle the XXXL** was lost at sea during an inner tube race. No successor could be found, triggering the **Biscuitant Deformation**, a series of power struggles that threatened to tear the Church asunder as rival groups claimed exclusive possession of the divine qualities of Flour Power required to assume control of the Papal Throne.

49 The *coup de grace* was delivered when undercover Clam Enemite hip-hop stars MC Goukouni Ramgoolam the Afrobot, Gerbilina the Chinchilla Thrillah, Porkmaster Flash, Sir Meta4 Mixalot, P Dudley-X, and DJ Dogg-E the Hip-Hop Hound, their astrolabes swinging around on giant gold chains, were elected Sextuple Popes in the year 512; within four years the Church was bankrupt and in ruins, due in no small part to their lavish *Cristal*-swilling lifestyles.[48]

---

[47] Many of these errant parodies of Biscuitism eventually came to be taken quite seriously. Indeed, over the subsequent millennia millions of people have killed each other while arguing over which religious parody they liked the most.

[48] In a desperate attempt to raise funds, the main BiscuiTemple was rented out to a medical group hoping to invent the field of *extremist podiatry* by making head amputations a common cure for ingrown toenails. Their logic was that one wouldn't feel the pain of an ingrown toenail once one's brainstem had been severed, plus the fact that the rapid metabolic shutdown following decapitation and death would prevent the ingrown toenail from getting infected. The cure never really caught on in popularity and so the BiscuiTemple rent went unpaid.

50 To make matters worse, over the generations the League's propaganda campaign had worked its insidious influence, leaving most people convinced that *the Church of Arglebargle itself was just some sort of a joke religion.* **The One True Religion**, the World's Oldest and Largest Biscuit Cult, which had once been the subject of nefarious parody was now *itself* considered the parody, while the joke religions were considered legitimate! Oh, to what a dismal state of apostasy humanity had fallen!

Pope Myron "Mango" Bartholomew the 23th, the eighth victim of the dreaded F.W.I. (*Flossing While Intoxicated*) curse

51 Due to this sorry state of affairs the loyal Biscuiteers were forced underground again. A small group ransacked the Library at Alexandria for plans, built rockets and then left for the stars, living on comets in the Kuiper Belt as the famous space-faring **Huguenauts**. Others stayed on Earth, forming the **Biscuitist Resistance Forces For The Liberation of Almost Everything**, led by the charismatic guerilla leader **Comrade Subcomandante "Sparky" von Ibn**.

52   The Biscuitist Resistance Forces For The Liberation of Almost Everything, often mistakenly referred to as the **Knights Templar**, were protectors of the Holy Grail, a petrified Biscuit totem left behind by a band of neo-Space Squid missionaries called the *Squid Squad*. The "Templars" worshipped this Biscuit as a manifestation of the God-Biscuit Hirself; when this fact was discovered in October 1307 the League in Support of Clam Enemas surmised the true purpose of the "Templars" and ordered them executed *en masse* by autoerotic defenestration.

53   Many Biscuitist brothers and sisters lost their lives in the resulting purges; following battles such as the Siege of Fort Whatchaduin, Biscuiteers were scattered like unto leaves before a brisk autumn wind. Some fled to England and Scotland, among the few places of sanctuary available, while others went to Asia to assist in mop-up operations after the catastrophic collapse of the notorious *Does Genghis Khan = An Imaginary Raisin?* experiment.

54   The Church went deep underground following this calamitous turn of events. With its power base scattered the Church was largely inactive in politics, though Biscuiteers still played prominent roles in the arts. For example, though most of the images of Biscuits have long since been painted over, Michelangelo's *Sistine Chapel* was once a lovely fresco telling the tale of God-Biscuit's first fishing trip, and the ensuing zany hijinks when everyone accidentally brought the baked beans to the subsequent *First Annual Angelopolis Fish Fry Potluck, Yard Dart Tournament & Wet Kirtle Contest*.

55   Another aesthetically influential *artiste* of the time was the noted Biscuitist auteur **Baron Cosimo de Giuseppe "Corky" von Boyardee the MCMLXIX[th]**, who wrote **God-Biscuit, The Musical:** *On Ice!*, which premiered in Venice on Monday, February 29, 1588. Despite rave reviews in all the trendiest madrigal fanzines of the day, Clam Enemite suppression has been so successful over the centuries that of the 427-song cycle, only one hymn remains:

Whisk It, Oh Biscuit
> Twenty-four dimensions
> With the curves to match
> Yo, it's the God-Biscuit
> S/He's quite a catch
>
> Take Hir out
> And party 'til dawn
> That Biscuit's flirtin' like mad
> God-Biscuit's got it goin' on.
>
> > *chorus* [*to be sung in a bel canto baritone*]
> > S/He's just a Biscuit
> > In Hir own groove
> > Just a Biscuit
> > Got Hir eyes on you
> >
> > S/He's just a Biscuit
> > Yo, S/He's in full effect
> > S/He's just a Biscuit
> > Don't mean no disrespect
> > Uh-huh!
>
> Flakin' that crust
> Like it ain't no thing
> Rippin' up the dance floor
> And a-flashin' Hir bling
>
> The night is steamy
> So around you S/He'll prance
> If S/He only had a lap
> S/He'd like a lap dance
>
> > *[chorus]*
>
> Kneadin' that Dough
> For hot 'n yeasty action
> Get some lovin' in the oven
> And some crusty satisfaction

Early next morning
Gotta take a shower
It's time to get clean
And rinse away the flour

[chorus x 2]

56   The first major event in the Biscuitist Renaissance happened in 1826, when the Church of Arglebargle deacon, **the Honorable Renfrew "Melvin" HeeHaw the Third,**[49] discovered America. The New World lay beyond the sunset, waiting to become the Arglebargle power base: After centuries of underground hibernation within the chrysalis of obscurity, the Church was ready to rise like the Phoenix of legend from the ashes of destruction and reassert its power on a global scale.

57   The rediscovery of the Americas was a turning point in the clandestine warfare between the League and the Church. "Discovered" in 1492 by Christopher Columbus, the New World was considered the land of opportunity by many people ready to start their lives anew. The discovery had caused quite a sensation throughout the entire civilized world, but Biscuiteers, distrustful as they are of the mass media/consensus view of reality, hadn't bothered to read the newspapers or ask anyone what all the commotion was about until 334 years later, when "Melvin" happened to strike up a conversation with a deck swabber in a grog hall.

58   Once the Church knew of the discovery it wasted little time in sending ships across the ocean to investigate potential baking opportunities. The first schooner met with disaster, sinking off the coast of Nova Scotia when it slipped on a floating banana peel and capsized. The second mission fared better, though the typist of the Dossier of Instructions had been eating *Cheetos* while typing, rendering the pages illegibly smudged with crusty orange smears. Struggling to interpret the greasy orange mission statement, the Biscuiteer puritans instead mistakenly ended up investigating the

---

[49] Figurehead of the Puritan Biscuitist sect known as **Melvinism**, and widely renowned as Mozart's favorite tambourine player.

growing possibilities of nuts and legumes, fortuitously paving the way for George Washington Carver to invent peanut butter over a century later.

59   The next truly major event in Biscuitist history didn't occur until January 8, 1935, when the Divinely-inspired Nuclear Platypus was once again brought forth into our world. Yea, the very Essence of the Glorious God-Biscuit was incarnate in human form once again, to return unto the masses the Flour Power of the Divine Dough! *Huzzah!*

60   Decked out in Hir favorite seersucker suit, God-Biscuit had realized the woeful state to which humanity had fallen, and how far away from Hir truth they were. It was Hir plan that the Nuclear Platypus, in **The Second Coming**, would rally humanity under the Biscuit Banner once again.

61   Integral to Hir plan was that Hir essence should manifest in the body of a solipsistic borderline sociopath, as such a person would be the last anyone would ever suspect of being a platypus in disguise, much less a *nuclear* platypus. Just to be safe, this new Doughist Messiah could admit to no one who He really was, not even to Himself, lest rival religions or Clam Enemites have Him assassinated, crucified, or pushed down a flight of very steep stairs.

62   Though the God-Biscuit is infallible, this, alas, was a bad idea. As Divine Plans go, 'twas a dud doomed to abject failure. The form chosen to be the Vessel of God-Biscuit was the myth, the man, the mammal, **Leroy "Wicker" Lincoln**.

CANTO VI

NEUTERONOMY
LEROY "WICKER" LINCOLN:
A LIFE COVERED IN FUZZ
A Cautionary Tale

Herewith articulating the spiritual desolation that looms large in a life of Biscuiteouslessness

1   No name reverberates across the history of western monoculture as does the name "Leroy 'Wicker' Lincoln." This enigmatic figure, this shadowy titan among men, this charismatic riddle of a biped has piqued the passion of the teeming masses like unto no other. Humans around the planet subconsciously demand to know the secrets of "Wicker," the mammal behind the myth.

2   What we know as a debatably incontrovertible fact is that "Wicker" was the secret brother of President Abraham Lincoln. Although born nearly one hundred years apart by different parents in different countries, and bearing only the most superficial morphological resemblance, genealogists consider Abraham and "Wicker" to be identical twins.[50]

3   "Wicker" was born in Ulan Bator, Mongolia in 1920 and moved to the United States in 1921 at the age of fourteen, ten years before His twentieth birthday in 1935, the Holy Year of His Birth. Because His body surged with the great powers of the Nuclear Platypus, *but He was denied the self-knowledge that He Himself was in fact the Nuclear Platypus incarnate in human form*, "Wicker" was a quite emotionally disturbed young man whose core concept of self-identity fluctuated wildly at the quantum level.

---

[50] Either that or "Wicker" was *The Notorious Worm Sphincter Speculator With an Ear of Corn Reclining on a Corn Cob Couch*, about whom you may have learned with shudders of anticipation/ dread during abstinence class in high school.

4 As a 22-year-old teenager He had the phrase *Wipe Your Troll* tattooed across His belly in large purple letters.[51]

5 As this gimmick lost its luster "Wicker" moved on to other parts of the world. It is from this point on that all evidence is little more than apocryphal hearsay. Some say that "Wicker's" personal evolution progressed along the same lines as that of a grape: as the years passed He changed from smooth and plump to wrinkled and small.

6 More average than usual and adrift in a quagmire of moral and gastronomic relativism, "Wicker" refused to acknowledge either the power of the God-Biscuit or the evil of the SpapOopGannopOlop. A lost, flustergastulated soul he was[52], yearning for meaning in a Doughless and Platypus-free world, without the boundaries of good or evil and lacking even ethics or decent breakfast options.

7 Selling collectible vintage air guitars and wearing His favorite crotchless clown suit, He wandered the railroad tracks north of San Miguel de Allende, Mexico, mainlining powdered skunk discharge. He suffered terribly while being relentlessly pursued by: (1) an armada of rabid chimps on the prowl for Thomas Jefferson, armed with enormous syringes full of lite beer; or, (2) a herd of half-herring half-human *manchovies*, their gill slits flapping wrathfully; or, (3) 40,000 hedgehogs and Boltzmann brains rotating in unison. In the grip of His paranoia "Wicker" never could ascertain precisely by whom He was pursued.

8 'Twas ever thus: Supporting Himself by selling the famous *Eager, Stressed-Out Leroy "Wicker" Lincoln Action Figure With Extendable Forehead, Disposable Chin & Two Free Dreadlocks*, "Wicker" spent years attending rural country fairs, picketing the judge's booth of the home-baked apple pie competition with signs that said, "Judge not, lest *ye* be judged." He was eventually banned from the fair, never to be heard from again.

---

[51] In His later megalomaniacal messianic phase, He paraphrased the tattoo as *Wipe Thee That Troll That is Thine*. In a later attempt to conserve vowels He had the tattoo changed to *Wp Yr Trll*.

[52] Flustergastulated = Flustered + Flabbergasted + Discombobulated

9   Shortly thereafter. "Wicker" founded the world's first sing-along suicide cult. Generally described as a Jonestown death camp crossed with the hit musical *Grease*, the cult prospered until 1947, when an alien spaceship crashed into their headquarters and destroyed all the Barcaloungers. Their varsity jackets and poodle skirts filthy after a day of slave labor in the fields, and now faced with a sudden lack of comfortable seating options, the distraught cult members frantically moseyed and/or sashayed off into the wilderness in search of cozier gulags.

10   After repeatedly filling out His income tax forms in Roman numerals, "Wicker" was thrown into jail, where He died of taco leg in 1956.

11   Meanwhile, frog.

12   Other experts say that a new and improved negatively-enhanced "Wicker" sweated profusely, dripping a thick, syrupy perspiration that smelled like fish. Stumbling through the courtyards of Missoula, Montana with systematic aimlessness, He gesticulated wildly while pleading for anyone to join Him in His favorite imaginary game *Meat Darts*, spraying alarmed passersby with His fishy discharge while driving heavy, primitive farm equipment at high speeds on dangerous mountain passes in the Swiss Alps, repeatedly yelling out, "Are *you* who I think *I* am?!?"

13   His attempt to coin pithy and hip slang phrases such as, *actin' like sausage*, or, *ipso facto, lhasa apso*, failed miserably, as the phrases inexplicably never caught on amongst the burgeoning recombinant American youth cultures of the day.

14   "Wicker," a veritable *übermensch* among tap-dancing bagpipe-playing soprano country-rapping phenomenological *bourgeoisie* philosophers of the great American heartland, made His debut on national television doing imitations of professional impersonators, duplicating feats of simulated mimicry with a genuine sense of mimetic authentic duplicity. Critics regarded his performance as thrillingly dull and gratuitously austere, with blatant subtexts of submissively aggressive mediocrity and obsessively laid-back spontaneous deliberation.

15 Nonchalantly headless, "Wicker's" television career ended when He outraged the nation by attempting to buy an umlaut from Vanna White on *Wheel of Fortune*. He was last seen attempting to design a self-sniffing armpit in preparation for the end of the world.

16 Some suspect that "Wicker" is the same man immortalized in American folklore as the *Rubber Urban Tumbleweed Tycoon*. Realizing that a largely urban populace rarely, if ever, comes into contact with the joy that is tumbleweeds, "Wicker" incorporated a mobile factory called *Rubbin Erber Tubberweem, Inc.*

17 Feverishly searching for His shadow with a solar-powered flashlight and engaging in systematized spontaneity; experiencing palatal diphthongization and trying out for the synchronized sniffing afrobat team by digitally inserting Himself into taped reruns of *America's Next Top Model*; proclaiming His opposition to *habeas corpus* based on an ill-conceived notion that it had something to do with necrophilia; suffering from delusions of adequacy; these were His pastimes as "Wicker" and His factory zigzagged randomly across the U.S. fabricating rubber urban tumbleweeds. Once completed, the rubber urban tumbleweeds were casually tossed out the back door when no one was looking. As the cities slowly accumulated rubber urban tumbleweeds, the kindness and philanthropism of "Wicker" was praised from sea to shining sea, as though it were because it is.

18 "Wicker" quickly squandered His fortune by setting up a media conglomerate front company in the Cayman Islands, producing derivative movies, plays and music. The company fared poorly overall, but the worst flops were:

- *Dong of the Dead*
- *So Long, and Thanks for All the Crabs*
- *The Curious Spectacle of the Lachrymose, Yet Still Interrogative, Wildebeest*
- *Krystallnacht on Sesame Street*
- *Alas, the Weevil Cried, "Adieu"*
- *Waiting for Gödel*
- *Honky-Tonk Troglodyte*
- *A Whiter Shade of Puce*

• *Something Twitchy This Way Comes*
• *Leonard in the Sky with Diamonds*[53]
• *Last Mango in Paris*
• *Tiny Tim: Live at Folsom Prison*
• *A Streetcar Named Pestilence*

---

[53] Lyrics e.g.,

> Picture yourself in a tricked-out Camaro
> With beige bucket seats and wood-paneled sides
> Somebody calls you and hands you a Big Gulp
> His lapels are incredibly wide
>
> His plaid leisure suit is in yellows and greens
> A two-liter Pibb in his hands
> Look for the man with the missing front tooth
> And he's gone
>
> > Leonard in the Sky with Diamonds
> > Leonard in the Sky with Diamonds
> > Leonard in the Sky with Diamonds
>
> Follow him into a shag-carpet trailer
> With air hockey tables and frozen pot pies
> Everyone smiles as you hand out the Fritos
> And baskets of chili-cheese fries
>
> Blocks of Velveeta appear in your hands
> Here, have some Miracle Whip too
> Slather some onto your white Wonder Bread
> And you're gone
>
> > Leonard in the Sky with Diamonds
> > Leonard in the Sky with Diamonds
> > Leonard in the Sky with Diamonds
>
> Picture yourself on a giant recliner
> With built-in drink holders and leatherette sides
> Suddenly someone is there with a mullet
> The man whose lapels are so wide
>
> > Leonard in the Sky with Diamonds
> > Leonard in the Sky with Diamonds
> > Leonard in the Sky with Diamonds

- *The Secret Agent from A.C.R.O.N.Y.M.*[54]
- *Matisse and the Spontaneous Warthog*
- *Billy-Fred: The Rock Opera*
- *I, Cooter*
- *Pseudomodo, the Backup Hunchback of Notre Dame*
- *Hop-Along Ocelot*
- *Hang Ten! Fifteen Great Waterboarding Tunes by the Beach Boys*
- *Leibniz vs. Newton: Clash of the Honkies*
- *Green Eggs and Hamlet*[55]
- *... and the Wind Cried, "Wally"*
- *The Cow that Bumped into the Moon*
- *Dial 'M' for Mucopolysaccharide*

---

[54] A.C.R.O.N.Y.M. = **A**rglebargle **C**oncept **R**eclamation, **O**ntology **N**egation, & **Y**east-based **M**inistry

[55] A representative excerpt:

> Alas poor Yorick,
> You did say,
> "Dost ye like green eggs and ham?"
> I say thee nay.
>
> I like them not in a field
> Nor at Elsinore Castle
> Green eggs and ham
> I do find a great hassle.
>
> What a piece of work
> Is this green egg with ham,
> Ophelia fixed me a plate
> I did say, "No thanks, ma'am."
>
> To eat or not to eat,
> That is the question,
> Of green eggs and ham
> I do vomit at the very suggestion.
>
> I like them not in a forest,
> Nor in town, nor in fen,
> I liketh *not* green eggs and ham,
> Not now and not then.

- *Winston Churchill: Blood, Sweat, Tears, and Buns of Steel*
- *R-E-P-U-L-S-E: Urethra Franklin's Greatest Hits*
- *I Weep for the Prognathous*
- *Un Chien de Maïs Andalou*
- *Fondle Me Elmo*
- *Accountantz in tha 'Hood*
- *Leningrad's Funniest Home Video Bloopers*
- *Adolph the Syphilitic Reindeer*
- *Shuffleboard Grudgematch: Robots vs. Alligators!*
- *The Legendary Lapse of Larry the Weepy Leper*
- *Kramer vs. Kramer vs. the Martians*
- *Whistle While You Wipe*
- *Sing Along with Snortley the Adenoidal Elephant*
- *Four-Fisted Wombat*
- *Lt. Flappy's Hermaphroditic Wheezing Gullet Band*
- *Spank My Gator at Goiter Gulch.*

The enterprise flopped horribly, "Wicker" went bankrupt, and so it is that the rubber urban tumbleweeds tumble no more.

19 A group of maggot wranglers in Rennes-le-Chateau, France, claims to have proof that "Wicker" knew of an impending alien invasion of Earth and became the first human to reach the moon in 1947.

20 These pupating French rabble rousers say that "Wicker" had a loose cavity filling that vibrated to the precise frequency of radio communication protocols used between rogue elements of the United States military and warlike, proctologically-obsessed extraterrestrial empires.

21 Able to hear their tinny, squeaky voices burbling forth evil plans from His stinky decayed tooth, "Wicker" built a rocket and blasted off with three tons of prepackaged preservative-laden snack food, hoping to save Himself from the imminent invasion.

22 Disoriented en route by an amino acid flashback, "Wicker" crash landed on the moon and began to suffocate. Thinking quickly, He used up the air in His bags of potato chips and pretzels, an air supply that lasted until July 1969. At that time members of the first officially-acknowledged moon landing arrested "Wicker" for trespassing, declaring

Him to be an enema combatant and incarcerating Him in a detention camp located deep beneath the polar ice cap. Genetic experiments later determined that "Wicker" had consumed enough Polysorbate-80 to live for at least 950 years.

From Monoculture to Unibrow: Leroy "Wicker" Lincoln, CEO of Counterfactual Entertainment Enterprises, Inc., during his days of glory as a power-player in the Military-Industrial-Entertainment Complex. Responsible for such flops as *Sniff My Tentacle* and *When Comb-Overs Attack*, "Wicker's" days as an entertainment mogul were deservedly short-lived.

23 Other researchers allege that "Wicker" was a set of orphaned hermaphroditic Siamese triplets with an Oedipus/Electra complex. Green Beret troops apprehended "Wicker," trying Him/Her/Them before a military court on charges predicated on the fact that pain hurts, demanding a minimum sentence of lifelong incarceration. One of the more coherent octopoid Jerry Lewis mutant clones executed "Wicker" on Labor Day 2047, an event that was broadcast live during Tribunal/Telethon Week, bringing in record donations for the cures of genetic disorders that typically afflict only cheaply-cloned octopoid Jerry Lewis mutants.

24 "Wicker" rose from the dead on the third day after His televised execution, cloning Himself from DNA traces in a stray toenail clipping He had found in a restroom ashtray at a bus station. Resurrected and ready to rock, He decided to become a beloved children's matinee idol. After months of radical surgery and cosmetic amputations, He made His debut

onstage as **The Bilaterally Symmetrical Pirate**, with both legs replaced by wooden peg-legs, each hand replaced with hooks, and eye-patches over both eyes. Alas, "Wicker's" first paying job as entertainer at a birthday party went horribly awry. He managed to stumble into the room avuncularly enough, but the combination of blunt wooden feet, blindness, and two sharp hooks took its toll: His shiny hooks flailed as He lurched His way across the crowded romper room, His wooden legs tripping over the *papier-mâché* donkey. The ensuing gruesome spectacle left the community traumatized for years to come.

Leroy "Wicker" Lincoln as
the beloved-by-few
Bilaterally Symmetrical Pirate.

25   Last but least is the version that most Arglebargle experts regard to be by far the least inaccurate account of the strange life of Leroy "Wicker" Lincoln, a veritable barnacle with a grudge trapped within a man's body.

26   In this variant of the legend, President Dwight D. Eisenhower commissioned "Wicker" to plan out the U.S. Interstate Highway system. Wearing naught but a penis sheath made of the finest sasquatch intestine, "Wicker" performed the job with zest, handing in the completed drafts to the President a full six months ahead of schedule. Army Corps of Engineers road crews quickly put the plans into effect.

27   However, no one knew the seething morass of God-Biscuitless antipathy and hatred that now swirled within "Wicker's" festering brain. A dejected life of aimless wandering in search of salvation, rejecting the glories of the Divine Dough as far too carbohydrate-laden, had scarred "Wicker" in body, psyche and soul. Hostility and resentment directed His every action in a mighty, booming voice that echoed throughout the walls of His corrugated cranium.

28   Burdened by neither talent nor charisma, "Wicker" was now fully unhinged from His already-negligible moral code. The pain of Biscuiteouslessness finally fully upon Him, he had come to regret that the feared alien invasion predicted by His rotten tooth had not come to pass. So, in His project for President Eisenhower, He had secretly designed the U.S. highway system to spell out "FREE ICE WATER" in the *lingua franca* of militaristic alien empires when viewed from outer space. This attempt to lure thirsty space aliens to Earth in mighty invasion fleets to decimate the human race was "Wicker's" lowest moment. Alas, 'twas doomed to failure.

29   [Allegations that "Wicker" manipulated continental drift itself so that the entire planet spells out *'Kreeble deeble snood, dude'* have yet to be satisfactorily substantiated.]

30   What "Wicker" had not anticipated was the fact that most aliens' metabolism was incompatible with the molecular structure of water: Ordinary Earth water makes non-squid space aliens explode, a basic fact of which "Wicker" was apparently unaware. Vacationing aliens began to avoid our planet altogether, breathing a sigh of relief that the warning was visible from so far away. Thus was the global economy not only spared vicious alien invasion fleets, but was denied valuable tourist dollars as well.

31   This titanic failure was the last straw. His vestigial tail tucked betwixt His legs, "Wicker" sought one last chance for redemption by joining the CIA, seeing a final opportunity for glory in the upcoming Cubist Missile Crisis.

32   Alas, tragedy struck once again. Unable to find the CIA's listing in the yellow pages, on March 24, 1957 "Wicker" went into what He thought was the U.S. Army. The group He joined, however, was in truth a front for the dreaded pro-SpapOopGannopOlopian organization, The League In Support of Clam Enemas, and had been laboring for millennia to return the SpapOopGannopOlop to our universe.

Eternal moral, spiritual and gastronomic desolation awaits those who live a life of Biscuiteouslessness.

33   By comparing dental record databases and artificial ingredients, the League had figured out "Wicker's" true identity and purpose. They kidnapped Him while He was on His way home from a wookie bris and took Him to their headquarters, a *Hooters* restaurant in a secret chamber hidden beneath the Great Pyramid of Cheops. Once there, they merged His body and a clone of Lee Harvey Oswald into a freshly-shaven albino sasquatch body and revealed to Him that His true father was Billy Carter, singer/guitarist of the acid rock band *The Billy Carter Experience* and brother of then-future President Jimmy Carter.

34   The Clam Enemites claimed to have proof that Billy Carter was a Martian elf-warlord who had migrated to Earth's North Pole for better unemployment benefits, and was mad that "Wicker's" offer of FREE ICE WATER had been a scam.[56]

35   Scholars are still debating whether these nefarious allegations about Billy Carter are true, but they were shocking enough to snap "Wicker's" mind and make Him vulnerable to brainwashing.

36   When His tour of duty in the "Army" was over, "Wicker", as the now-brainwashed Nuclear Platypus in a freshly-shaved albino sasquatch body, was let loose upon the world in service to the League In Support of Clam Enemas.

37   He performed many covert duties, the most famous mission being the time that "Wicker", Lee Harvey Oswald, Billy Carter, and James Dean (also brainwashed by the League and reincarnated as the Loch Ness monster) pretended to kill John F. Kennedy (who was really the Lindbergh baby) so they could transplant JFK's brain into the body of Big Bird, who would later appear many times on *Sesame Street* making eloquent speeches to children about the importance of cooperation and civic duty.

38   "Wicker" did many things undercover, evil missions now classified at the highest levels of government secrecy. Suffice it to say, these nefarious deeds were designed to further the goals of the League In Support of Clam Enemas and set up the conditions necessary for the return of the SpapOopGannopOlop.

---

[56] It has been suggested by in-house Arglebargle psychologists that Billy Carter's militaristic anger and aggression were the result of insecurity and low elf-esteem.

39   Finally, in August 1977, one of two events occurred.

40   In the first scenario, which is unlikely yet probable, "Wicker" overdosed on *Preparation H* and became a gaseous mass with a tendency toward raging homonecrobestiality, existing simultaneously in all clothes dryers in the universe and eating socks without fear of reprisal.

41   Many scholars rule this first scenario as false and claim that scenario two is much more probable yet unlikely: God-Biscuit broke through the Nuclear Platypus's brain-washing and called Him back, for the mission had failed. "Wicker" staged His "death" to fool the League and left Earth in a flying saucer to rejoin the ranks of the Doughy Hosts.

42   So it is that "Wicker" still roams the universe in a UFO driven by His adorable squid chauffeur Buckley, trying to undo the evil that He unknowingly perpetrated.[57]

43   "Wicker's" actions on Earth had set in motion a chain of events that were closing in rapidly, but of those you will read in the next chapter, for my time of writing is finished.

44   In the words of the God-Biscuit, "I am Them, Them I am, and Them's all that I am. Except when I'm not."

WANTED
FOR BLASPHEMY
THE EPILEPTIC AARDVARK

Hey kids! Don't end up like *this* guy!
Praise the glory of the God-Biscuit
BEFORE IT'S TOO LATE!

---

[57] Either that or He lives in your clothes dryer and eats your socks.

CANTO VII

BISQUITUS

Herewith chronicling in terrifying detail BisQuitus, the horrifically horrendous, totally apocalyptic and reality-wrenching end of the world

55   Behold! Thou dost readest the revelation of **I, the Omniscient** (who am myself, but whose name doth slippeth past me at the moment), which God-Biscuit gave unto me to show Hir creation THAT WHICH HAS ALREADY COME TO PASS BUT HAS NOT YET HAPPENED.

54   The time is at hand, but the hand is gone and time lingers no longer. We are in the *No Age*, naught more than the remnants of a residual reality that has long since moved on to better things.

53   Reality itself, all of the firmament, the land, the sea, and all things that walk, crawl, dash, slither, skate, frolic, swim, glide, mope, stomp and/or ooze upon/within it, hath already gone through the **BisQuit**, the apocalyptic eschaton, the end of all things.

52   This subject of which I speak is true: *the end of the universe has already happened.* Aye, but the end happened so quickly that the rest of the universe is still trying to catch up, not realizing that it no longer exists.

51   Following is an explanation of how I know of this:

50   'Twas Bloomsday morn as I sat by the bubbling brook in the meadow near the monastery, strumming my lyre with a plectrum. I had just finished brushing my tooth[58] and was chanting *The Ditty of the Doughbala*:

> In days of hardship, in times of strife,
>> oh God-Biscuit be the light that guides my life.
> As I look to the heavens I huzzah and rejoice,

---

[58] Having found that it's easier to take *great* care of one tooth than it is to take merely *good* care of 32 teeth.

oh God-Biscuit, lend me Thy voice.
To blaspheme against Thee, I dare not risk it,
  for you are my inspiration, oh Glorious God-Biscuit.
Your golden Dough, 'tis only You I love and trust,
  oh God-Biscuit, how I long to peel Your flaky crust.
When I think of Thee mine heart goes a-flutter,
  oh God-Biscuit how I yearn to slather Thee with
  butter.

when I did hear from behind me a voice most strange, as of a llama choking on corn chips.

49   The choking voice managed to gurgle out: "I am the antecedent to Myself. I am Yin and I am Yang. I am the All in Each. I am This, That and the Other. I am Alpha and Omega, the First who is Last. And verily forsooth, this very sentence that I now utter doth not be true, so get thee not thine pantaloons wadded up into a bunch."

48   I turned to see the source of that voice which spake unto me and I did behold a pug-ugly albino horse, and the name that sat upon it was **Festus**, who did say, *Eat at the Festus Poop Deck: Seafood specials daily!* Behind Festus I did see seven half gorilla/half lobster hybrids, and lo!, they were bouncing on pogo sticks. They sproinged and tumbled about, gaily falling upon one another.[59]

47   Behind them was a shack with a sign tacked on, and yea that sign did say, "Gone ghotion." From out of the door and into the midst of the annoyingly perky lobsterillæ came the most beloved of God-Biscuit, aye the Nuclear Platypus Himself, in a form reminiscent of the pinnacle of cucumber evolution. And lo!, He did set aside a fishing pole.

46   The Messianic Monotreme did have a head and snout that defied all rules of perspective, and He was colored like unto the color of a chameleon standing on a mirror. His eyeballs were bulging in and out of His head as if spring-mounted to a trampoline inside His skull, and first the left eye would bulge and retract, and then the right eye would bulge

---

[59] Due to the inherent difficulty in grasping the handlebars with their huge hairy claws, mayhap 'twas difficult for them to balance while bouncing.

and retract, alternating rapidly in sequence over and over and over. His skin was like unto that of extra-crispy fried chicken, and He was excreting bean dip out of all of the pores upon His blessed body. Through the translucent fleshy bits of His webby flippers I could see faint flashes from a mesh of alternate realities across the omniverse.

45 This Platypus most Nuclear had in His right hand something that was neither a noun nor a verb, and in His left hand He caressed an aperiodic pentagonal tessellation. From His mouth converged an array of butterflies that were playing the song *Celebration* by Kool & the Gang on harmonicas, a blessed spectacle known as the Harmonica Convergence.

44 As I gazed on in wonder He grunted, sprouting a tentacle from deep within the depths of His firkin and waggling the crispy, fleshy proboscis at me in salutations, portending portentous portents.

43 Turning phlegmy rumblings into an effective means of communication, He gurgled at me in binary code, like unto a computer spewing forth mucus from its power port. Showing signs of possible zygomatic flexure, He said unto me, "Come with Me, you whose name slips past Me at the moment. The end is nigh and I, the all-knowing and all-seeing Nuclear Platypus, doth wish for a chronicler of the deeds that shall take place."

42 I grabbed His tentacle and with His lobsterillæ in tow we fell up to an armada of pre-owned UFOs, all emblazoned roundabout with God-Biscuit decals and totally pimped out with seven-wheel positraction, homie hoppers, dual-quad V-8 fuel-injected engines, bucket seats, fuzzy dice, ZK60 mag wheels, and enormous swaying udders.

41 Awaiting us on board the chief UFO were Merle Haggard and Gregor Samsa; Aldous Huxley; Mason Reese; Irving Forbush; Fuzzy Dunlop; Henry David Thoreau; June Carter Cash; Diamond Dave Whitaker; a wildly random, fluctuating assortment of Sweathogs and Flying Burrito Brothers; Jimmy Hoffa; Godot; Syd Barrett; Chester Cheetah; Frank Stella; Lenny & Squiggy; Deleuze & Guattari; Georges Braque; Jerry Cornelius; Ralph 124C41+; A Boy Named Sue; Luther Blissett; Hierocles and Philagrius; Oliver Cromwell; J.G. Thirlwell; Susie Chapstick and Suzy Creamcheese; Clard Svensen; Daniel Boone; Pat Hearn; Robert Fludd; John Wesley Harding; Joseph Simonton; Noam Chomsky; Arnold Ziffel; Troilus and Criseyde; W.G. "Snuffy" Walden; Giordano Bruno; Johnny Ryall; Lucas "Snapper" Carr; Horselover Fat; Peyton Manning and Bob Loblaw, Esq.; Konstantin Wagenheim; Judge Judy; Mr. Bradley Mr. Martin; Bilinda Butcher; Flat Stanley; the Harlem Globetrotters and the weeping women of Euripides; Doiby Dickles; Dora the Explorer; Douglas Adams; Ferris Bueller; the Captain & Tennille (before they went commercial and sold out); Bucky Fuller; Letha Weapons; the 742nd Annual Ontario Podiatrists Convention; David Foster Wallace; Robert Anton Wilson; Christian Rosenkreutz; R. Mutt; Flex Mentallo; John Zerzan; Beowulf; Harry Smith; Jesus;[60] BJ & the Bear; Chuck Dukowski; and Jimmy Carl Black, the Indian of the group. The flight crew consisted of James Bond and Forrest Gump.[61]

40 Powering the UFOs with their propellers were rayon-based homomorphic self-encrusting snotbots that had (just

---

[60] Whose name spelled backwards is *susej*, indicating that he is a *sausage* Biscuit.

[61] When these two first met it went something like this:
  "The name is Bond... James Bond."
  "Hi, I'm Forrest... Forrest Gump."

barely) evolved from the lowly and revolting Oozumgreep of chapter three.

39   After an in-flight showing of *Weekend at Bernie's II*, the Nuclear Platypus simultaneously came to each and every one of us with a tray. Upon the tray sat a plate of Biscuits and a Klein bottle, and He did say unto us, "Eat thee of this Biscuit, for It is My Body, and drink ye from this chalice of gravy, for it is My blood."

Ask not for whom the Biscuit bakes; it bakes for THEE.

38   After we had each blissfully taken part in the communionication with the Platypus of Power, yea verily the Quasi-Mammalian Monotreme of Might, He did take me aside to communicate verbally via micromodulation of pressure waves in the atmosphere.[62] Speaking under strict conditions of anonymity, the Nuclear Platypus did say unto me this:

---

[62] In other words, He talked.

37 "These are the Prophecies of Things Past, the Retro-Prophetic Future-Memories of Past Events to Come.

36 "When the end is/was drawing near, Liberace will launch his **Meat-Seeking Moisture Monkey** at a 7,000-foot-tall Engelbert Humperdinck effigy in the Bermuda Triangle.

35 "Without provocation, there will be an epidemic of exploding cows in an attempt to accelerate the destruction of the biosphere of the planet Earth.[63]

34 "A seven-headed pterodactyl will go clubbing in Pyongyang and phototropic slugs with excess cellulite will ripple gelatinously with the coming of the dawn.

33 "Something vaguely resembling an autistic nine-legged hang-gliding tarantula riding a unicycle *with a periscope* will challenge world political leaders to roll enchiladas with a chainsaw while playing nude Twister™. It will be discovered to be an overeducated and sesquipedalian supersonic iguana named **Flad** trying to impersonate itself and lo!, it will have lips composed of its own lips.

32 "It will be discovered by Earthling scientists that the sun is a nuclear-powered kumquat, resulting in, of all things, widespread lard worship as worshippers genuflect greasily and shout, 'Praise the Lard!'

31 "Incredibly large armadas of walking catfish will terrorize the Northern Hemisphere, demanding acupuncture while randomly obliterating fast-food franchises.

30 "An egg will accidentally be elected President of the United States as the result of a hitherto-unnoticed flaw in the electoral process, only to become the first known victim of *Political Assassination By Boiling*. And behold, the assassin's motto shall be, 'Why impeach when you can poach?'

29 "When it is discovered by the liberal media that a mere egg had been elected to direct the course of western civilization, and not only that, but the egg in question was boiled in the Oval Office by an intern and that *no one noticed*, chaos will reign worldwide and civilization itself will teeter on the brink of collapse.

---

[63] Please refer to 'Appendix VIII: The Horrific Truth About Paperclips, *Revealed at Last*'

28 "'Twill then be discovered that the paperclip is in truth all of humankind's subconscious suicidal urges condensed into a convenient office utensil that signals the end of human evolution.[64]

27 "Then shall appear the final sign of things to come: The advent of he who be known as **EepSpeepGoopOloop, *the Diabetic Cannibal*,** a shriveled and putrescent fellow who shall bear the name *Schmuckulus*, and who doth be the dreaded **Corpulent Bondage Frog**, evil step-nephew and second-cousin thrice-removed of the Paradise Frog. Upon a 400-square-mile Etch-a-Sketch he shall twiddle out his motto, *Religion is the laxative of the masses*, causing much wailing and gnashing of teeth.

26 "With the wretched EepSpeepGoopOloop will the SpapOopGannopOlop finally succeed in putting forth Its seed into our universe once again, for verily forsooth is this EepSpeepGoopOloop the earthly manifestation of the most wretched SpapOopGannopOlop!

25 "Obsequious Earthlings, enraptured by the alluring Siren Song of the SpapOopGannopOlop, will flock to the evil EepSpeepGoopOloop, he who doth be the **Anti-Platypus**.

24 "The Biscuiteers, believing members of the Church of Arglebargle and the Chosen Ones of the God-Biscuit, will see through the deceptions of the EepSpeepGoopOloop, but alas 'twill be too late. The EepSpeepGoopOloop and his lieutenants most foul, the *Kornberger*, *Korkberger* and *Squirtberger*, will force one and all to wear foam-rubber hamburgers. Alliance with the EepSpeepGoopOloop shall cause the dreaded *EepSpeepGoopOlooperosis*, in which the victim's entire right brain hemisphere dissolves, turning the youth of America into blank-eyed Zom-B drones, merrily dancing a farandole and addicted to the will to power.

23 "Then, distraught at winning only 4th place in an air guitar contest at the Vladivostok Glee Club's Biennial Cabbage/Pancake Dinner, the miserably croaking voice of the EepSpeepGoopOloop will speak the SpapOopGannopOlop's

---

[64] Please refer to 'Appendix VIII: The Horrific Truth About Paperclips, *Revealed at Last*'

name **BACKWARDS, *ON ACCIDENT***, and so the Groined Vault of Infinity will reverse itself, unfolding outward so that the SpapOopGannopOlop will walk our universe again!

22   "In all haste will the God-Biscuit send Me, the Nuclear Platypus, to Earth.

21   "Verily this will be **The Third (and Final) Coming**, and I will descend down from the heavens to join My disciples for **The Last Supper**.[65] Finally, after **The Last Dessert**[66] we will join together in a rousing battle song, playing glockenspiels, mellotrons, Theremins, standup bass and Sousaphones, subtly punctuated with a delightful marimba glissando and accompanied by an infantry division of qawwali-singing clog dancers. Yea, our brutal battle cry will echo down the generations and strike fear into the hearts of Our enemies forevermore:

> Aye, the Dough Divine
> is doing fine
> up there 'pon the mountaintop
> Get there thee
> and you will see
> Hir smite the SpapOopGannopOlop

> For 'tis the hour
> of Flour Power
> and God-Biscuit's righteous glare
> The End is at hand
> so *here* we stand
> (though some stand over there)[67]

---

[65] A round of superb mini-quiches for *hors d'oeuvres*, followed by braised quail in juniper berry sauce and grilled asparagus drizzled with extra virgin olive oil, masterfully prepared by My personal chef François, topped off with a few amphorae of *Colt 45*.

[66] A yummylicious apricot soufflé.

[67] Several battalions of Ped Xing partisans will sing Her marching song too:

> Ped Xing, Ped Xing, Bo Bed Xing,
> Banana Fana Fo Fed Xing,
> Fee Fie Mo Med Xing,
> Ped Xing

20   "Having thus been summoned, the God-Biscuit will emerge into our reality, an orchidaceous *haute couture* masterpiece in a plus-size *Givenchy* poodle-skirt ensemble reminiscent of the 1980s revival of the 1970s' retro-'50s craze, with a positively darling handbag from *Louis Vuitton.*

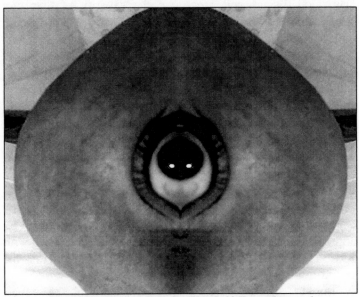

Behold thou one and all, *The Self-Excreting and All-Seeing Eyeball* **of St. Kory Huckleberri-Nut Vern the Last, Ph.D., and gesticulate accordingly.**

19   "Having spent the evening swilling mead, shaking it like unto a Polaroid picture and bar-hopping between **Studio 54** and **Area 51**, God-Biscuit will have on some major beer goggles. Totally crunk, S/He will espy a passel of migrating tree sloths and, intrigued and aroused to see them licking their own eyeballs to keep them moist, S/He will eagerly lurch over to get in on the action. And yea verily will the tree sloths scatter in sexual revulsion to all the four corners of the world.

18   "Feeling rejected, and seeing at last the devastation wrought in the wake of the SpapOopGannopOlopOlist minions, S/He will overturn Hir 40-ouncer of *Mead Malt Liquor Lite*, dumping it 'pon the ground and, slurring Hir words with a *jejune* insouciance, S/He will say, 'This mead I pour atop the curb for My homies; alas, we'll always have ArglebargleOpolis—'

17 "Grabbing Hir, I discreetly take God-Biscuit aside and sober Hir up a little, and lo!, noting with disdain that the SpapOopGannopOlop doth be wearing white after Labor Day, God-Biscuit will recognize the severity of Our dire circumstances. Having exacerbated an old slam-dancing injury while out clubbing, and after 470 bazillion years finally beset by tennis elbow, hot flashes and a developing bald spot, S/He will be sore and cranky, only partially sober, and *Most Fearsome to Behold.*

16 "Manifesting in Hir terrifying aspect of divine wrath, **Doughzilla BeelzeBiscuit, the Varmint of Vengeance and Judgmental Yeast Beast of Apocalyptic Judgment** [*sic*], God-Biscuit shall rage hither and thither with an obvious hankerin' to whup some SpapOopGannopOlop booty.

15 "S/He will rally together all of the members of the Doughy Hosts, reminding them that, 'I am the Alpha and the Omega and don't you forget it.' They shall descend from on high like unto the valkyries of old, locked & loaded with TABs.[68] Flame and fury will abound as they charge across the sky in mighty Biscuitron 5000 battle-chariots, bringing forth swarms of synchronized assault lobsters. Joining covert Biscuitist operatives like *Biobot and The Third Person*,[69] the mighty *Thrice-Baked Hermes and His Refried Beings, Doktor Bobo the Simian Semiotician and His Howling Prime-8 Platoon*, the fearsome *Alchemy Bomb of Mnemonaut, Abstractus and the Sphinxter*, the grim and gritty *Militant Haardvark, the Public-Access Possum,* and *Alliterative Lass,*

---

[68] Tactical Assault Biscuits

[69] The Third Person tended to annoy people with its movie star-like tendency to speak of itself in the third person, saying things like, "As far as The Third Person is concerned, The Third Person prefers to speak of The Third Person in the third person," and so on, driving its erstwhile comrades *Millie Miracle* and the *Mammal Master* positively batty from pronoun deprivation. Incidentally, The Third Person's teen sidekick, *The Second Person*, was institutionalized after years of speaking of itself in the second person led to severe identity crises and self-confidence issues.

plus *the Split Infinitors & Pumblechook Sweedlepipe, the Onomatopoeic Monomaniac*, the Hosts will do battle with the odious SpapOopGannopOlop and Its vile groinbot minions.

14 "The sky will crack, white will become black, inside will fuse with outside and Quxxxzxxx will flex his spleen, but alas 'twill be too late.

WARNING: OBJECT ON PAGE MAY BE CLOSER THAN IT APPEARS

What, Me Worship?: After a night of bar-hopping betwixt *Studio 54* and *Area 51*, the Glorious God-Biscuit totally jumps the shark when S/He shows up drunk for the Apocalypse.

13 "Wearing a XXXXL t-shirt bearing the slogan, *It's A SpapOopGannopOlop Thing, You Wouldn't Understand*, the SpapOopGannopOlop will provide rampaging hordes of car-wash attendants with glow-in-the-dark four-dimensional meat players. Yea, they will play mumblety-peg and vomit in all directions roundabout, revving up their lawnmowers to create crop circles that spell out *Overall there's a smell of fried, dehydrated wombat colons* in Sanskrit.

12 "Then shall the Paradise Frog appear between the molecules behind the front of the bottom of the top of our

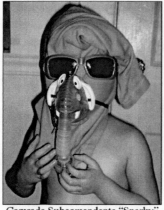

Comrade Subcomandante "Sparky" von Ibn, the world's zaniest jihadist

backs, attempting to eat his own mouth and demanding that no one obey him. And behold: the Paradise Frog shall be in his vengeful apocalyptic aspect of **THE FINAL FROG!**

11 "The God-Biscuit and the Final Frog will prepare to merge once again into the Rudimentary Kumquat, thereby reopening the Groined Vault of Infinity and banishing the vile SpapOopGannopOlop back to whence It came.

10 "At the crucial moment of Groined Biscuit-Frog metamorphosis, however, a machine will float down from the sky, emerging from the supercontext and trailing a banner that doth say *Excessive worrying should be cause for concern*. And lo!, from the machine shall emerge a godlike form, a *second* Nuclear Platypus! 'Tis My faster-than-light bifurcated self from Chapter Two, paragraphs **8-10**! Dressed in an excessively baggy Hawaiian shirt, He will become quite confounded and out of place upon spotting Me, and lo!, He shall be laden with cheese. My/Our surprise will be mighty indeed as I/We stare at My-/Ourself!

9 "Speaking in raw qubits, My doppelganger shall say unto Me, 'Whoooooa dude, I been, like, lookin' all over for you, bro! So yo, like does this bunion look infected or what? It's like discolored or somethin' — '[70]

---

[70] It wasn't so much that the bunion was infected or discolored, but that His aft starboard flipper had been tattooed lime green during a long-forgotten night of drunken revelry, an evening of Dionysian merriment involving the time-lost Nuclear Platypus 2.0, the bumpkinish-but-vaguely-likeable Nucular Platypus, two 5-gallon buckets of *Vick's VapoRub*, Quxxxzxxx's inbred cousin/grandpa Quqaqzqaquq, and nearly 30,000 liters of low-sodium lobster bisque. Plus hazy memories of Bigfoot riding a unicorn at a rodeo.

8   "Turning toward the source of a calamitous noise, I shush Myselves in horror. My/Our duckbills gape in fear as I/We note that in the confusion caused by My time-lost Self's arrival, the SpapOopGannopOlop has taken advantage of God-Biscuit's semi-sloshed and inhibited reaction time to neutralize the reopening of the Groined Vault of Infinity!

7   "Yea, the SpapOopGannopOlop will whip out cans of aerosol *Dough-B-Gon* and *Ribbit-Inhibitor* to forcibly divide the God-Biscuit and the Final Frog, disrupting the Groined Biscuit-Frog Fusion Process at its most crucial juncture! The trans-universal equilibrium will be unbalanced and lo!, everything that exists and does not exist will be destroyed and re-created simultaneously, a veritable Phoenix on a universal scale!

6   "To make things even more blasphemous, at the last femtosecond the SpapOopGannopOlop will take a bite out of the God-Biscuit's blessed Biscuitoid body, chewing lustily with Its moldy, halitosistic teeth!

5   "After this final indignity, what is now the universe will be fused into a single dimensionless point of Divine Dough, caffeine, and frog legs. Yea, in truth 'twill be an infinite celestial armpit with multi-faceted compound eyes like unto a bug, and It will watch Itself as It sniffs Itself, and sniff Itself as It watches Itself sniffing and watching, and verily forsooth shall this lead into **The Blessed 1,000,000 Billennia of Watchful Self-Sniffing**, and S/He who is now God-Biscuit will then truthfully be **Dog-Biscuit**, the result of the great anadromic *Roll Reversal.*

4   "Mind you, all that I have said has already happened, but like the Argle Froggle Spapple 'twas over before it began, so the universe is trying to accommodate the resulting loophole in the timestream, not realizing that *it has already fallen into that loophole and long ago ceased to be.*"

3   After the Nuclear Platypus finished His revelation, we stood in silence for a few moments. Sensing that these apocalyptic visions had left me flustered and stressed, He waddled over nonchalantly and led me to a nearby waterbed to give me a sensuous massage. He seduced me with His gurgling, phlegmy breath, which was hot and heavy as He

111

whispered sweet nothings into my ears. His darting tongue was like a wriggling, spasmodic earthworm as it flecked in and out of His cartilaginous snout, tickling my earlobes with quick, slimy little slurps. The warts, pimples, moles, ticks and scabs on His hairy back tickled my fingers as I dug my fingernails into the clammy cellulite of His midsection. His eyes glittered like pools of iridescent blue mucus beneath a full moon, sparkling with delight as He tantalizingly peeled off His loincloth and traced tender figure-8s in the small of my back with His well-manicured, silky flippers. The fat reserves in His flap-like tail jiggled and throbbed with ecstasy as I nibbled playfully on the moist, rubbery gristle between His webbed toes, and His endothermic sweat glistened like droplets of ambrosia beneath the steamy, clinical glare of the UFO examination room lights. Our breathing grew more tense and rhythmic as the waterbed rippled under the passion of our grunting, heaving bodies.[71]

The aftermath of the apocalyptic 'Roll' Reversal: From God-Biscuit to Dog-Biscuit, one third of the triune *Celestial Self-Sniffing Armpit of the Infinite Afterlife*.

2   Later, after about thirty seconds of spooning, the Nuclear Platypus bid me adieu and disappeared from my sight. I lay back to ponder the imminent and/or preceding apocalypse when suddenly the UFO flight crew burst into the room. After Mr. Gump had given me an obligatory rectal probe they dropped me off on the side of the turnpike, with nary a *Stuckey's* or payphone in sight, and flew off into the sky, the inconsiderate bastards.

---

[71] Dial **(555) PLATYPORN** for more *Hot Platypus Action*!

1   Though like you I do not exist, I have faith that what the Nuclear Platypus hath anonymously told me is true. Open your mind to the God-Biscuit and live your life to the absolute fullest, for soon time will catch up to itself and we will immediately (d)evolve into a universal armpit with compound eyes like a bug that watches Itself sniff Itself for a million billennia,[72] and the Each shall be as the Entirety, at last truthfully one with the God-Biscuit, body and soul.

0   And so, unto you I have naught to say but this: In this universe you have to be crazy or you'll go insane. Amen.

And so 'tis written:
HERE ENDETH THE HOLIEST OF BOOKS

THE
NUCLEAR PLATYPUS
BISCUIT BIBLE

TRANSLATED FROM THE ANCIENT TEXTS

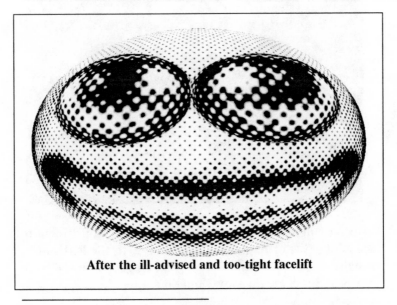

After the ill-advised and too-tight facelift

---

[72] It looks like Leroy "Wicker" Lincoln got it right for once! (See chapter six, *Neuteronomy*, paragraph 15 for more info.)

THE CHOICE IS YOURS!

Wilt thou endure an eternity of
SpapOopGannopOlopOlist Agony?

Wilt thou deny the Deity of Dough and risk banishment to
the Lint Mills of Arglebargle, or worse, to the loathsome,
roughage-free Hobbesian blight and chigger-infested back
alleys of SpapOopGannopOlopOlis?

THE CHOICE IS YOURS!

THE CHOICE IS YOURS!

Wilt thou live a festive and/or mirthful eternity
of Biscuitoid Bliss?

Wilt thou accept God-Biscuit into thine heart (or at least thine stomach)? If such be the case, oh humble critter, prepare thyself for delights undreamt as you frolic gaily through the Golden Fields of Earwax in Heavenly bliss!

THE CHOICE IS YOURS!

115

APPENDICES

APPENDIX I

HOW TO VISUALIZE THE GOD-BISCUIT

We here at Arglebargle Global Headquarters are bombarded day and night with earnest enquiries about God-Biscuit. A misconception that underlies many questions is that we are talking about a regular "biscuit," the type one might buy or barter at a restaurant or store.

Please allow us to be blunt so as to prevent further misunderstanding: **Store- or restaurant-bought corporeally manifest "biscuits" are naught but pathetic imitations of the infinite grace, ectoplasmic elegance and aerodynamic magnificence of a true Biscuit.** This type of "biscuit," *a mere three-dimensional food item*, must always be written in lower-case letters or spoken of in an ironic tone (with air quotes) to show that you're not fooled by its shallowness, falsity, and generally pathetic, over-eager, trying-too-hard, wanna-be-Dough desperation.

Rather, when we speak of Biscuits we refer to those Biscuits that exist in the spiritual realms, the noumenal realms, and at the extreme outer boundaries of conceivable mathematical, ontological, epistemological and conceptual models. These Biscuits are One with God-Biscuit in their common Biscuiteousness, but are separate and singular entities, whereas God-Biscuit is All of Everything. S/He is the Fundamental Biscuit of Reality, a self-replicating, binary, gluten-based, self-baking biocosmic fractal algorithm that created the universe as an experiential matrix resulting from the existential tension generated by Hir desire for stimulating conversation.[73]

To clear any residual misconceptions we will attempt to describe God-Biscuit for you: S/He is a vision beholding itself. S/He is the absence of nothing, devoid of voids. S/He is the lack of the lack thereof. S/He is the true color of a mirror.

If none of these concepts help, let us try an alternate, less poetic explicatory method: Imagine a dot (•); that is *one* dimension. Now look at a flat image like a drawing or a photograph; that is *two* dimensions. What we appear to live in and perceive is three spatial dimensions plus one temporal dimension, for *four* dimensions.

Now simply picture an infinitely large expanding Biscuit that occupies, manifests, consists of, and comprises our 4-D reality multiplied by six (= *twenty-four* dimensions) and you will have just envisioned God-Biscuit. Double-check the verisimilitude and accuracy of your vision against the evidentiary image on the next page, if necessary.

If that doesn't work try this: Imagine something so incredibly wonderful and overwhelmingly complex that you can't even imagine it. Are you imagining it? If so then you're doing it wrong, because *we told you to imagine something so wonderful and complex that you can't imagine it*. Try again.

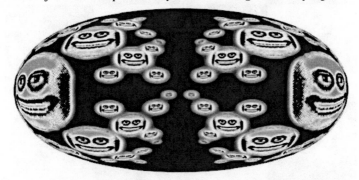

A recent photograph from the Deep Space Telescope mission, showing the inflationary expansion of the early universe. The above image documents events from one zillion-bazillionth of a microjiffy after the 'Big Bang' (aka the *Burstin' Biscuit*).

---

[73] Or at the very least, juicy gossip.

Check the verisimilitude and mimetic accuracy of your vision of the God-Biscuit against the evidentiary image shown above.

APPENDIX II

MATHEMATICAL PROOF OF THE EXISTENCE OF THE GOD-BISCUIT

Assign God-Biscuit a mathematical value of **A**, and the universe a value of **B**. **A=B+A**, because God-Biscuit is the universe but the universe is and is not God-Biscuit.

Add **A** to **B+A**, divide by **1** plus the square root of **-1**, to which we assign a value roughly equivalent to zero exponentially raised to the zeroeth power, multiplied by **B-A** minus *phi* to the 11,011[th] digit, which we will call 0^0/**C**.

A is now equal to 0^0/**C** + **B(AΦ)‹A**. The geometric representation of this equation suggests the shape of a circle. Simply square the circle and convert the resulting square into an equilateral triangle with **A** as the base, **B** as the altitude, and 0^0/**C** as the hypotenuse.

Remove the base (**A**), combine the altitude (**B**) with the hypotenuse (0^0/**C**), assign to **B+0^0/C-A** a value of **1**, multiply **1** by **A** and the result is **A**, which is the assigned value of the God-Biscuit. *Quod erat demonstrandum*

In visual terms:

B + A ÷ 1 + 0^0/C + B(AΦ) ‹A = ● = ■ = ▲

- A = B + 0^0/C – A = 1 x A =

Q.E.D.

APPENDIX III

THE NATURE OF PHYSICAL REALITY

The nature of physical reality can be quite difficult to understand, yet very simple to comprehend.

The problem that immediately comes to mind in terms of grasping the nature of physical reality is the fact that *nothing actually exists*, as was irrefutably proven in the Introduction to this book.

To get around this problem one must realize that since there is *so much* 'nothing' that it has the same qualities as 'something'. One cannot determine what "nothing" is unless one can compare it to "something," because nothing is a relative concept. Since nothing exists there is no something, and no something also means no nothing.

In other words, assume nothing to be a void; a void can exist only if there is something to compare it to and/or an observer to note its status as a void. However, if something and/or someone exists then it is by definition not a void.[74]

As was proven in the Introduction, there is no universe, so nothing exists, which is a lack of something. It has just been proven that nothing cannot exist without something (and vice versa), so a lack of something means an absence of nothing, and *an absence of nothing implies and necessitates the presence of something*.

Ergo, the very existence of the universe proves that it is impossible for the universe to exist, which proves that it is impossible for the universe to *not* exist, thus guaranteeing the existence of the universe.

In other words, the universe does exist, the universe does not exist, the universe does and does not exist, and the universe neither does nor does not exist (and vice versa).

---

[74] An axiom long known by ontological cosmologists as the *Void Avoidance Strategy*.

APPENDIX IV

THE NATURE OF BODILY AND SPIRITUAL EXISTENCE

All of your life you have probably believed that you have a body. *You are wrong.*

"You" quite conceivably exist, but "your" body doesn't. That may come as something of a shock, but you must pull away the veil of illusion and face the truth: Everything that comprises "you" and "your" body is in actuality nothing more than a thought-projection of your spleen. For the spleen is, in fact, an insertion-point into our reality, like a cursor on a computer screen; it is a biophysical gateway through which hyperdimensional intelligence bleeds into our universe. Many of you have long suspected that this is the case, and now, at last, your suspicions are verified!

The spleen is the *true* center of consciousness and is the most highly evolved life form in the universe, but has no means of movement. For billions of years on thousands of planets spleens struggled to cope with this handicap. Flopping about in the alien soil, annoyed, they eventually evolved a mastery of mind over matter: Using psychic energy vibrations to control the atomic and molecular manifestations of matter around them, they formed "bodies" for use as a method of transportation from one point in space/time to another.

Life forms on occasion have their spleens surgically removed; this sounds like a terrible ordeal but is in actuality easily dealt with. As stated previously, the spleen is highly evolved: It exists in various forms in 18 of the 24 local dimensions, so its removal from this plane of reality weakens it a bit but leaves it none the worse for wear in the long run.

Eventually your spleen will discorporate, resulting in the "death" of your body as the spleen decoheres and leaves the physical realms altogether. In the blessed post-life realms the residual energy traces of your spleen (aka your "soul") will be hunted down and eaten by the **Space Bruthas From Beyond The Stars**. The Space Bruthas will metabolically convert your spleen into gaseous n-dimensional radio waves, which they will emit via P2P data-encrypted aetheric **Trans-Galactic Hemorrhoidal Communication Transmissions**[75] to your proper place in the Afterlife amid the quaint neighborhoods, boroughs and bungalows of Arglebargle the AbodeBiscuit.

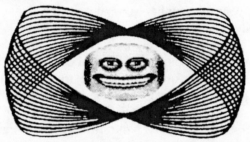

God-Biscuit using Hir mighty powers of rectal telepathy to alchemically emit the vibratory frequencies of Hir Eternal Doughy Love to all the neighborhoods of the universe.

---

[75] Trans-Galactic Hemorrhoidal Communication is a form of high-frequency, rapid-burst rectal telepathy used by nearly all forms and cultures of space-faring extraterrestrial intelligence. Precisely-pulsed hemorrhoidal telepathic transmissions act as a common language among the many interstellar races, a sort of sphincter-based *Esperanto* of galactic empires, if you will.

The DNA code can sense when a particular species is nearing the stage of space migration, and accordingly provides that species with hemorrhoids upon attainment of an appropriate level of Biscuito-spiritual readiness and technological sophistication.

Hemorrhoids are the most effective, reliable and high-bandwidth means of interspecies communication ever developed, though they are admittedly subject to occasional painful signal surges due to solar flares and sunspot activity. If such a signal overload occurs, the aggrieved individual or species should consult a pharmacist or communications specialist who can fine-tune the "antennas."

APPENDIX V

A CONCISE PRIMER ON THE RELATIVITY OF SPACE/TIME

Of the 24 dimensions of Apparent Reality that were created from the 24 dimensions of the God-Biscuit, twenty are curled up in infinitesimally small Calabi-Yau manifold superstring form, like stringy dough made by an ill-equipped baker. There are three unfolded spatial dimensions: width, length, and height. The spatial dimensions are interesting because, like floors and walls, if you change their positioning their properties change too. If you take a long stick from the ground and stand it upright it's no longer long, it's tall; lay it down sideways and it's wide.

Another interesting aspect of our local universe is the concept of *time*. Time flows continuously from one point to another, and thus is both digital and analog. It may be easier for the layperson to think of this in terms of the relationship that exists between one point in time and another point in time. For example, now we think of then as then and of now as now, but then we thought of then as now, although then was then now and now was then then. In other words, then was now, then, and now was then, then, though now is now now and then is then now. To clarify this, what was now then, is then now, thereby implying that now is now, now, but then was now then, then. You must also remember that then is not then then, but then is now but not then then, just as now is not then now, even though it was then then, when then wasn't then, but was now (then).

Generally speaking, most life forms take for granted that one can see or recollect the past, but few believe in the ability to see or remember the future. In fact the past and the future are different polarities of the same thing ("now") that just happen to be flowing in opposite directions. Just as you cannot have a left side without a right side, you cannot have a past without having a future; they are both simply different and relative aspects of the Eternal Now.

To remember the future one should see the future as the past in the future, and the present as the past of the future past in the future future. The future of the present is best discovered as the past of the future, but the future of the present, or the present of the future past, the present of the past future (or past present, if you prefer) is the past in the future and the present future in the past.[76] To sum up, what is now the past was then present in the present/now (then), when what is now the present (the past future [then]) was then the future but is now the present now and yet the past of the future now, which is now then but will then be now in the present future and present past future (then).

Here, however, is where things can get confusing: Einstein proved that space and time are symmetrically interwoven and should be treated not as space and time, but as *space/time*: When now [= time] in the present here [= space], which was then the future there/then in the past here there then, the past was then here now (i.e., there and then) but now then (now) here, and the present here then and there, but now here[77] will someday there and then be here and now in the present future (here then but then now, there in the present future then), and now here (not to mention now then) in the past/future seen then as future/past, there in the present past then seen now here [space] as the present future then, when and where it will there then in the present past [time] be *here* at last.

---

[76] It goes without saying, then, that the past of the present is also the past of the future but not the past of the past, but the present of the past *in* the past, when it was the present that contained its own past which was a past of the past present which was the present then but is now the present past.

[77] Recall, though, that the *Heisenberg Uncertainty Principle* necessarily limits the degree of specificity to which one can know precisely when and where here and now is relative to then and there.

APPENDIX VI

WIN A NIGHT OF HORROR IN AN OUTHOUSE!

This test is administered to evaluate your biophysical and neurocognitive compatibility with the rigorous demands of the Biscuitoid lifestyle. Entries must not be filled out and submitted by August 9, 2969.

1. Why are you not other than as you are? _____
2. What is your favorite autonymic word that implies itself and is what it means? (Circle one)
   (A) Word (B) Polysyllabic (C) Noun (D) This
3. Is your answer to Question # 3 *really* correct? Yes_ No_ All of the above_ (Explain) _____
4. Jet-lagged hamsters should not perform rhinoplasties while piloting space shuttle missions. True_ False_
5. Can you confirm that your answer to this question will not be "yes"? Yes_ No_
6. Is one *really* a carnivore if one only eats vegetarians?
7. What did you think about *that*? _____
8. Why not two semi-chewed fish sticks smeared across the faded asphalt of a parking lot, being slowly desiccated by the sun? _____
9. *Really?* _____

10. Do you like this question? (You can level with us, it won't hurt our feelings. Seriously.) _____

11. C'mon, really: What did you think of question 10?

12. Not to sound *clingy* or *obsessive*, but seriously: ***did you like question 10 or what?!?*** _____

13. Please write a one-word question suitable for a test of this nature and then answer it using one word or less.

14. In your estimation, do aardvarks like polka music?[78]

15. If you took all the blood vessels out of a person and stretched them out end-to-end they would extend all the way to the moon and back; more importantly, *that person would die.* 0% maybe_ 100% maybe_

SERVING SUGGESTION

---

[78]   This is not a question to be taken lightly; recent studies indicate that yes, aardvarks do have quite an appreciation for polka music. The average aardvark, upon hearing high-decibel polka tunes, shows noticeable signs of joy, glee and/or mirth as the aardvarkian **Polka Perception and Appreciation Instinct** kicks in. This enjoyment, however, is a double-edged sword: the more polkas an aardvark hears *the more it wants to hear.* What started as ecstasy turns to agony, and soon the once-happy aardvark roams the streets with the peculiarly dead eyes endemic to polka addicts.

    A nocturnal mammal in this state can be quite dangerous to confront; if your aardvark becomes increasingly aggressive while pestering you to buy an accordion, then submit the aardvark in question posthaste for evaluation by trained authorities. One should exercise all due caution and keep emergency numbers nearby. Be prepared to utilize tasers, tear gas, water cannons and other crowd control measures if circumstances warrant.

<u>Multiple choice [use a #2 pencil to check the correct answer]</u>:
THE ABOVE IMAGE IS:

_(A)   **All of the above.**

_(B)   **A glimpse into the very substructure of reality, the foundations of space/time where squarks and superstrings vibrate and shimmer within the aether... where statistical discontinuities bubble up through the quantum foam to create the architecture of actuality, where chaos and order intertwine, mingling amongst the Doughist Archons and the abstract substrata of mathematics, metaphysics, and symmetry *to weave the souls of all who live.***

_(C)   **Ryan Seacrest's subjective interiority.**

_(D)   **Stick your hand up there and twist until it pops, fold the flaps over twice, rinse and repeat.**

APPENDIX VII

HOW TO UNDERSTAND APPENDIX VII

This sentence begins with a large and rather grandiose **T**. This is the second sentence, which you will read immediately prior to reading the third sentence. If you were a speed-reader you would have finished reading Appendix VII by now. This sentence has you under its control for the moment because you will continue reading it until it has nothing left to say.

This sentence marks the beginning of a brand new paragraph. This sentence refers to the fact that this sentence refers to the fact that this sentence refers to itself. Do not plagiarize this sentence, under strict penalty of prosecution. Apparently this is a sentence that exists only to point out that it exists as a sentence rather than existing as something else.

This sentence appears elsewhere in Appendix VII. It is not necessary to read this sentence.[79] This sentence is misplaced. The previous sentence happens to be false, as is this sentence, but the following sentence is true. If the meanings of "true" and "false" were switched then this sentence wouldn't be false. Do not read or obey this sentence. Against all odds, it just *had* to be this sentence. Information theorists are ambivalent about the qualities and capabilities of this sentence. This sentence refers only and always to all sentences that do not refer to themselves. This sentence is content-challenged, lacking a certain richness of descriptive ability.

This sentence is composed of a complex network of semiotic symbols that comprises an information-transference

---

[79] Nor is it necessary to read this footnote.

system based on the differential tension generated by the arbitrary nature of the signifier-signified relationship, which the author of Appendix VII is manipulating erratically. This sentence makes you think of the God-Biscuit. This sentence refers to no other. This sentence is short.[80] This sentence contains a hidden meaning. So does this sentence. This sentence is struggling to make do with the meager fifteen words allotted to it; oops, make that nineteen. This sentence is so smooth it's practically writing itself. This sentence is terse.

This sentence almost appeared in a different paragraph of Appendix VII, but got stuck here instead at the last minute. This sentence would be completely different if it were not self-referential. This sentence appears elsewhere in *The Nuclear Platypus Biscuit Bible*. This sentence is the thought you are currently thinking. If you are not reading this sentence please feel free to ignore it. Feel free to quote this sentence. This sentence pompously belittles old-fashioned and extroverted sentences that refer to things other than themselves. *This sentence is italicized in an attempt to seem youthful, daring and vivacious.* This sentence syntactically is challenged syntactically, and redundant too.

This sentence appears elsewhere in Appendix VII. This sentence ain't be grammar too good, but hopes to got gooder English someday. This sentence is self-nullifying. This sentence hereby secedes from itself and only appears once in Appendix VII. This sentence lasts only until the period at the end. (This entire sentence is little more than a parenthetical insertion.) This sentence declares itself to be the last sentence in Appendix VII, but be forewarned that a notoriously unreliable narrator wrote this sentence. This sentence forgot the point it was supposed to make, so never mind. This sentence is a pointless digression. Ten words ago this sentence had not yet started. ~~This sentence is a victim of censorship~~. This final sentence isn't actually a sentence because it has no period at the end

---

[80] This footnote is gratuitous and unnecessary.

APPENDIX VIII

THE HORRIFIC TRUTH ABOUT PAPERCLIPS, *REVEALED AT LAST*

Throughout history many fearsome things have posed a threat to the survival of the human species. None, however, has been quite so dangerous as the mind-numbing menace of the paperclip.

While most people agree that, for example, the threats of bioterror plagues and nuclear planetary genocide are indeed terrifying, the same people fail even to recognize the calamitous menace of the **paperclip**. In blissful ignorance humans call them mere "paperclips," not realizing that these **Weapons of Mass Convenience** are all of mankind's worst fears manifest as seemingly harmless office utensils.

Unbeknownst to most office workers, paperclips (*Papyrus clyppicus*) were created on the planet Earth in ages long past. Dastardly minions of the SpapOopGannopOlop landed approximately 23,517 years ago and altered the genetic structure of a group of bovine quadrupeds (aka *cows*), mutating their DNA from *deoxy ribonucleic acid* to *deoxy paperclipeic acid*, cloning the cows to look like paperclips.

These **Mutated Bovine Quadruped Paperclips** lay inert in sleep mode for millennia, awaiting only the invention of paper so they could strike and insinuate themselves into the quotidian fabric of day-to-day human life. Since then they have multiplied quickly, and have already reached a population guesstimated by Preemptive Cliptology Experts to be roughly 943,261,715,674.29.

The threat of paperclips manifests on the Earthly plane via the following three dangers:

1   Since paperclips are actually mutated cows in disguise, they contain the mass of a cow densely packed into

the very small size of a paperclip, giving them very powerful gravity fields. As paperclips appear in greater numbers Earth's gravity will become increasingly distorted. Eventually the planet will either break away from the sun's gravitational pull and go careening wildly out of control through the galaxy, or *Earth will implode into a black hole*, irrevocably altering and possibly destroying our sector of the universe.

2   Being cows, paperclips flatulently emit 200 to 400 quarts of methane per day. This methane rises into the upper levels of the atmosphere and depletes the ozone layer, contributing to catastrophic global climate change that will eventually destroy our planetary biosphere.

3   The shape of the common 'Gem style' paperclip is a sort of recursively in-turned and squashed oval-spiral shape, as can be readily ascertained through careful observation and intensive study of the image below:

A "paperclip"

This shape has no effect on the conscious mind, but in the subconscious mind it instills a need to imitate the shape of the paperclip and go in circles (figuratively speaking), making no progress and remaining stagnant. In those already prone to psychological fragility, the paperclip's inwardly recursive squashed-spiral shape is known to foster tendencies toward defeatism, narcissism and solipsism. *If unchecked, the invasive ubiquity of paperclips within humanity's natural habitat will cause genetic and societal evolution to grind to a halt, resulting in the extinction of the human race.*

Humanity could simply destroy all of the paperclips, but unforeseeable psychic damage may result. Studies indicate that humans have already become dependent on paperclips for subliminal guidance and for the convenient clipping together of documents. Without paperclips humanity would become directionless; extinction would result from the mass suicide of a species with a feeling of having "no place to go," and "no direction in life."[81]

The most obvious solution is to use genetic reverse-engineering to create a paperclip with a positive shape that promotes (a) free thought, (b) forward direction, (c) happiness, and (d) a general *carpe diem* neophilia. This would solve problem #3 but not problems 1 and 2, and so must be considered little more than a good start.

While it is too early to panic yet, the reader is advised to be vigilant around paperclips. Be particularly alert for the resonant sound of a tiny, chipmunk-like 'moooooooooooooooo' that seems to echo mournfully as if from across a distant field on a humid summer morn. If you hear such a noise be forewarned and take heed: it is the battle cry of a paperclip herd that feels threatened and is swarming to attack mode.

Please donate generously to your local Arglebargle BiscuiTemple's aggressive anti-paperclip youth initiatives, such as *Don't Be a Dip: Be Hip and Nip the 'Clip*. With your help we can mitigate the threat of the paperclip, a grave danger that permeates our lives and the very biosphere itself. As Benjamin Franklin said in 1759, "He who would sacrifice his liberty for the convenient clipping-together of documents deserves neither liberty nor convenience."

---

[81] Not to mention the widespread annoyance and environmental damage as the planet became inundated by loose, scattered and unclipped documents fluttering about.

**<u>Huzzah</u>! Ped Xing wants you to FLEX YOUR SPLEEN and do
your part against the paperclip menace!**

APPENDIX IX

THE CHARLIE DANIELS CODE:

The Glorious Doughist Secret Encoded Within Absolute Reality!

The arcane truth behind Biscuitism has long been known by a select few, the Ascended Masters of the planet Earth.[82] From the oral traditions passed down by firelight in the glottal tongues of Proto-IndoBiscuitoidian, to the sticky Dough orgies during the forbidden Rites of Eleusis in ancient Greece, to the very tome you now hold in your hands, the power of Biscuitism has inspired the masses of humanity for millennia untold.

However, as articulated earlier there are some who would keep the truth from the masses of humankind. SpapOopGannopOlopOlist forces such as the League in Support of Clam Enemas are intent on keeping humans from the radiant, soul-forging heat of *The Great White Light of the Oven on High*. In the event of catastrophe the truth has finally been encoded in a manner that guarantees it will be passed down from initiate to initiate for as long as the torch of Biscuiteousness burns brightly deep within the center of the human soul, thanks in large part to the efforts of **The Charlie Daniels Band**.

To start with, the very name of the band itself encodes a great secret, being an acrostic that carries a message of hope verifying that, whatever persecution a loyal Biscuitoid Mutant may undergo at the hands of Clam Enemites and other dastardly scoundrels, the Glory of the

---

[82] Ascended Master = *She or He For Whom The Dough Has Risen*

134

God-Biscuit shall reign supreme over the forces of Anti-Biscuitism hereunto forevermore:

The
Heavens
Embody a

Complex
Heuristic
Algorithm
Replicating
Love
In
Eternal

Dough,
Allowing the
Nuclear Platypus to
Infinitely
Exterminate the
Legions of the
SpapOopGannopOlop.

Behold the
Almighty, thee and thine, the
Nuclear Platypus and
Dough Divine.

This nigh-overwhelming and powerful message of inspiration drove the plot of the James Bond film *Platypussy*, but once Clam Enemite culture warriors realized what was happening the movie was pulled from theaters and all prints of the film were destroyed.[83] (The only existing copy is a partial reel now under guard within the vast suppository of

---

[83] This was a great cultural loss, as *Platypussy* was a wonder to behold: Sean Connery playing Bond, who is possessed by the SpapOopGannopOlop's Bandicoot Brigade, in tense hand-to-flipper combat against the very Nuclear Platypus Himself (masterfully played by the guy who played *Alf*) atop the escaped Multiple Monkey Mound adrift in the Bering Strait.

knowledge in the archives of the BiscuiTemple vault on the isle of Æaea, shelved next to DVDs of the banned television series *2001: Gilligan's Apocalypse*.[84])

However, we digress, so back to the urgent matter of the Charlie Daniels Code: In addition to the acrostic encoded within the name of the band itself, the very name "Charlie Daniels" was cleverly designed by Arglebargle Reality Technicians to be an anagram of "I called a shrine", reminding devout Biscuitist pilgrims to reach out to their local BiscuiTemple in times of need.

As is now obvious, the design of the entity known by humans as **The Charlie Daniels** is epistemologically and hermeneutically multilayered indeed. The aforementioned notwithstanding, by far the most important aspect of The Charlie Daniels Entity is the manner in which the deep

---

[84] *2001: Gilligan's Apocalypse* was widely shown in syndication until Clam Enemite censors figured out the theme song's lyrics and banned it posthaste:

> Sit right back and you'll hear a tale
> a tale of the universe
> where God-Biscuit worked to defy
> the SpapOopGannopOlop's curse.

> The mighty Nuclear Platypus,
> the Divine Dough's right hand man,
> Smites all heretics left and right
> It's God-Biscuit's plan.
> God-Biscuit's plan.

> The tree sloth with no eyelids could not
> keep his eyeballs moist
> the Platypus smote the Mass of Cheese
> and Biscuiteers rejoiced.
> Biscuiteers rejoiced.

> "Reality" ended long ago
> surely that is what you're thinkin',
> just be glad that you are you
> and not Leroy "Wicker" Lincoln.
> Not Leroy "Wicker" Lincoln.

structure of the universe itself is encoded within the popular song *The Devil Went Down to Georgia*. In this song the Devil (obviously a lackey of the SpapOopGannopOlop) goes to Georgia (an area renowned for the quality and quantity of Biscuits 'n gravy), whereupon said Devil is soundly defeated by the virtuoso fiddle-playing skills of a vernacular violinist infused with the ambient radiousness of Biscuitism.

Besides cryptically allusive and allegorical lyrics such as a "chicken in the bread pan pickin' out Dough" at the end of the chorus, stripping the lyrics of their base humanist affectations of *bourgeoisie* comprehensibility reveals the song's secret core message. *By reading the lyrics in* **binary code**, the manner in which The Charlie Daniels Entity originally wrote them, *one can see what The Charlie Daniels' agenda* **really** *was*: The use of binary code will allow *The Devil Went Down to Georgia* to be understood by peoples of the distant future after millennia of linguistic drift, or by space-faring extraterrestrial races that pick up radio waves of the song as it broadcasts out beyond the rim of our home galaxy 11,000 years from now. Encoding the song back into 8-bit ASCII binary code reveals a secret embedded at the very deepest levels of human cognition, woven into the quantized substrata of Total Reality itself.

The binary translation of the song (which begins on the next page) is composed of exactly 6,896 ones and 8,734 zeroes:

$$6{,}896 + 8{,}734 = 15{,}630, \text{ and } 15 + 6 + 3 + 0 = \underline{\mathbf{24}}$$

$\underline{\mathbf{24}}$ = God-Biscuit, *a* $\underline{24}$-*dimensional Biscuit.*

Furthermore,

$\underline{24}$ breaks down to $2 + 4$, and $2 + 4 = \underline{\mathbf{6}}$

$\underline{\mathbf{6}}$ = The precise number of syllables comprising the holy name *Nu•cle•ar Pla•ty•pus.*

Once you have recovered from the shock of the information revealed above, please refer to the translation that follows to verify these facts for yourself.

Encoded for the enlightenment of Biscuiteers, post-humans, and alien civilizations that use a base-10 system as the foundation of their mathematics, we are humbled to present The Charlie Daniels' greatest accomplishment:

APPENDIX IX.I

The Devil Went Down To Georgia:
The Binary Code Translation

O1010100   01101000   01100101   00100000   01100100   01100101
01110110   01101001   01101100   00100000   01110111   01100101
01101110   01110100   00100000   01100100   01101111   01110111
01101110 00100000 01110100 01101111 00100000 01000111 01100101
01101111 01110010 01100111 01101001 01100001 00001101 00001010
01001000 01100101 00100000 01110111 01100001 01110011 00100000
01101100 01101111 01101111 01101011 01101001 01101110 00100111
00100000 01100110 01101111 01110010 00100000 01100001 00100000
01110011 01101111 01110101 01101100 00100000 01110100 01101111
00100000 01110011 01110100 01100101 01100001 01101100 00001101
00001010 01001000 01100101 00100000 01110111 01100001 01110011
00100000 01101001 01101110 00100000 01100001 00100000 01100010
01101001 01101110 01100100 00001101 00001010 00100111 01000011
01100001 01110101 01110011 01100101 00100000 01101000 01100101
00100000 01110111 01100001 01110011 00100000 01110111 01100001
01111001 00100000 01100010 01100101 01101000 01101001 01101110
01100100 00001101 00001010 01000001 01101110 01100100 00100000
01101000 01100101 00100000 01110111 01100001 01110011 00100000
01110111 01101001 01101100 01101100 01101001 01101110 00100111
00100000 01110100 01101111 00100000 01101101 01100001 01101011
01100101 00100000 01100001 00100000 01100100 01100101 01100001
01101100 00001101 00001010

01010111 01101000 01100101 01101110 00100000 01101000 01100101
00100000 01100011 01100001 01101101 01100101 00100000 01110101
01110000 01101111 01101110 00100000 01110100 01101000 01101001
01110011 00100000 01111001 01101111 01110101 01101110 01100111
00100000 01101101 01100001 01101110 00001101 00001010 01010011
01100001 01110111 01101001 01101110 00100111 00100000 01101111
01101110 00100000 01100001 00100000 01100110 01101001 01100100
01100100 01101100 01100101 00100000 01100001 01101110 01100100
00100000 01110000 01101100 01100001 01111001 01101001 01101110
00100111 00100000 01101001 01110100 00100000 01101000 01101111

138

APPENDIX IX.I: THE DEVIL WENT DOWN TO GEORGIA:
THE BINARY CODE TRANSLATION

```
01110100 00001101 00001010 01000001 01101110 01100100 00100000
01110100 01101000 01100101 00100000 01100100 01100101 01110110
01101001 01101100 00100000 01101010 01110101 01101101 01110000
01100101 01100100 00001101 00001010 01010101 01110000 00100000
01101111 01101110 00100000 01100001 00100000 01101000 01101001
01100011 01101011 01101111 01110010 01111001 00100000 01110011
01110100 01110101 01101101 01110000 00001101 00001010 01000001
01101110 01100100 00100000 01110011 01100001 01101001 01100100
00100000 01100010 01101111 01111001 00100000 01101100 01100101
01110100 00100000 01101101 01100101 00100000 01110100 01100101
01101100 01101100 00100000 01111001 01101111 01110101 00100000
01110111 01101000 01100001 01110100 00001101 00001010

01001001 00100000 01100111 01110101 01100101 01110011 01110011
00100000 01111001 01101111 01110101 00100000 01100100 01101001
01100100 01101110 00100111 01110100 00100000 01101011 01101110
01101111 01110111 00100000 01101001 01110100 00001101 00001010
01100010 01110101 01110100 00100000 01001001 00100111 01101101
00100000 01100001 00100000 01100110 01101001 01100100 01100100
01101100 01100101 00100000 01110000 01101100 01100001 01111001
01100101 01110010 00100000 01110100 01101111 01101111 00001101
00001010 01000001 01101110 01100100 00100000 01101001 01100110
00100000 01111001 01101111 01110101 00100000 01100011 01100001
01110010 01100101 00100000 01110100 01101111 00100000 01110100
01100001 01101011 01100101 00100000 01100001 00100000 01100100
01100001 01110010 01100101 00100000 01001001 00100111 01101100
01101100 00100000 01101101 01100001 01101011 01100101 00100000
01100001 00100000 01100010 01100101 01110100 00100000 01110111
01101001 01110100 01101000 00100000 01111001 01101111 01110101
00001101 00001010 01001110 01101111 01110111 00100000 01111001
01101111 01110101 00100000 01110000 01101100 01100001 01111001
00100000 01100001 00100000 01110000 01110010 01100101 01110100
01110100 01111001 00100000 01100111 01101111 01101111 01100100
00100000 01100110 01101001 01100100 01100100 01101100 01100101
00101100 00100000 01100010 01101111 01111001 00001101 00001010
01000010 01110101 01110100 00100000 01100111 01101001 01110110
01100101 00100000 01110100 01101000 01100101 00100000 01100100
01100101 01110110 01101001 01101100 00100000 01101000 01101001
01110011 00100000 01100100 01110101 01100101 00001101 00001010
01001001 00100111 01101100 01101100 00100000 01100010 01100101
01110100 00100000 01100001 00100000 01100110 01101001 01100100
01100100 01101100 01100101 00100000 01101111 01100110 00100000
01100111 01101111 01101100 01100100 00001101 00001010 01000001
01100111 01100001 01101001 01101110 01110011 01110100 00100000
01111001 01101111 01110101 01110010 00100000 01110011 01101111
01110101 01101100 00001101 00001010 00100111 01000011 01100001
01110101 01110011 01100101 00100000 01001001 00100000 01110100
01101000 01101001 01101110 01101011 00100000 01001001 00100111
```

01101101 00100000 01100010 01100101 01110100 01110100 01100101
01110010 00100000 01110100 01101000 01100001 01101110 00100000
01111001 01101111 01110101 00001101 00001010

01010100 01101000 01100101 00100000 01100010 01101111 01111001
00100000 01110011 01100001 01101001 01100100 00100000 01101101
01111001 00100000 01101110 01100001 01101101 01100101 00100111
01110011 00100000 01001010 01101111 01101000 01101110 01101110
01111001 00001101 00001010 01000001 01101110 01100100 00100000
01101001 01110100 00100000 01101101 01101001 01100111 01101000
01110100 00100000 01100010 01100101 00100000 01100001 00100000
01110011 01101001 01101110 00001101 00001010 01000010 01110101
01110100 00100000 01001001 00100111 01101100 01101100 00100000
01110100 01100001 01101011 01100101 00100000 01111001 01101111
01110101 01110010 00100000 01100010 01100101 01110100 00001101
00001010 01000001 01101110 01100100 00100000 01111001 01101111
01110101 00100111 01110010 01100101 00100000 01100111 01101111
01101110 01101110 01100001 00100000 01110010 01100101 01100111
01110010 01100101 01110100 00001101 00001010 00100111 01000011
01100001 01110101 01110011 01100101 00100000 01001001 00100111
01101101 00100000 01110100 01101000 01100101 00100000 01100010
01100101 01110011 01110100 00100000 01110100 01101000 01100101
01110010 01100101 00100111 01110011 00100000 01100101 01110110
01100101 01110010 00100000 01100010 01100101 01100101 01101110
00001101 00001010

01001010 01101111 01101000 01101110 01101110 01111001 00100000
01110010 01101111 01110011 01101001 01101110 00100000 01110101
01110000 00100000 01111001 01101111 01110101 01110010 00100000
01100010 01101111 01110111 00100000 01100001 01101110 01100100
00100000 01110000 01101100 01100001 01111001 00100000 01111001
01101111 01110101 01110010 00100000 01100110 01101001 01100100
01100100 01101100 01100101 00100000 01101000 01100001 01110010
01100100 00001101 00001010 01000011 01100001 01110101 01110011
01100101 00100000 01101000 01100101 01101100 01101100 00100111
01110011 00100000 01100010 01110010 01101111 01101011 01100101
00100000 01101100 01101111 01101111 01110011 01100101 00100000
01101001 01101110 00100000 01000111 01100101 01101111 01110010
01100111 01101001 01100001 00100000 01100001 01101110 01100100
00100000 01110100 01101000 01100101 00100000 01100100 01100101
01110110 01101001 01101100 00100000 01100100 01100101 01100001
01101100 01110011 00100000 01110100 01101000 01100101 00100000
01101100 01110011 00100000 01110100 01101000 01100101 00100000
01100011 01100001 01110010 01100100 01110011 00001101 00001010
01000001 01101110 01100100 00100000 01101001 01101000 00100110
01111001 01101111 01110101 00100000 01110111 01101001 01101110
00100000 01111001 01101111 01110101 00100000 01100111 01100101
01110100 00100000 01110100 01101000 01101001 01110011 00100000
01110011 01101000 01101001 01101110 01111001 00100000 01100110

APPENDIX IX.I: THE DEVIL WENT DOWN TO GEORGIA:
THE BINARY CODE TRANSLATION

01101001 01100100 01100100 01101100 01100101 00100000 01101101
01100001 01100100 01100101 00100000 01101111 01100110 00100000
01100111 01101111 01101100 01100100 00001101 00001010 01000010
01110101 01110100 00100000 01101001 01100110 00100000 01111001
01101111 01110101 00100000 01101100 01101111 01110011 01100101
00100000 01110100 01101000 01100101 00100000 01100100 01100101
01110110 01101001 01101100 00100000 01100111 01100101 01110100
01110011 00100000 01111001 01101111 01110101 01110010 00100000
01110011 01101111 01110101 01101100 00101110 00001101 00001010

01010100 01101000 01100101 00100000 01100100 01100101 01110110
01101001 01101100 00100000 01101111 01110000 01100101 01101110
01100101 01100100 00100000 01110101 01110000 00100000 01101000
01101001 01110011 00100000 01100011 01100001 01110011 01100101
00001101 00001010 01000001 01101110 01100100 00100000 01101000
01100101 00100000 01110011 01100001 01101001 01100100 00100000
01001001 00100111 01101100 01101100 00100000 01110011 01110100
01100001 01110010 01110100 00100000 01110100 01101000 01101001
01110011 00100000 01110011 01101000 01101111 01110111 00001101
00001010 01000001 01101110 01100100 00100000 01100110 01101001
01110010 01100101 00100000 01100110 01101100 01100101 01110111
00100000 01100110 01110010 01101111 01101101 00100000 01101000
01101001 01110011 00100000 01100110 01101001 01101110 01100111
01100101 01110010 01110100 01101001 01110000 01110011 00001101
00001010 01000001 01110011 00100000 01101000 01100101 00100000
01110010 01101111 01110011 01101001 01101110 01100101 01100100
00100000 01110101 01110000 00100000 01101000 01101001 01110011
00100000 01100010 01101111 01110111 00001101 00001010

01010100 01101000 01100101 01101110 00100000 01101000 01100101
00100000 01110000 01110101 01101100 01101100 01100101 01100100
00100000 01110100 01101000 01100101 00100000 01100010 01101111
01110111 00100000 01100001 01100011 01110010 01101111 01110011
01110011 00100000 01110100 01101000 01100101 00100000 01110011
01110100 01110010 01101001 01101110 01100111 01110011 00001101
00001010 01000001 01101110 01100100 00100000 01101001 01110100
00100000 01101101 01100001 01100100 01100101 00100000 01100001
00100000 01011011 01110011 01101001 01100011 01011101 00100000
01100101 01110110 01101001 01101100 00100000 01101000 01101001
01110011 01110011 00001101 00001010 01000001 01101110 01100100
00100000 01100001 00100000 01100010 01100001 01101110 01100100
00100000 01101111 01100110 00100000 01100100 01100101 01101101
01101111 01101110 01110011 00100000 01101010 01101111 01101001
01101110 01100101 01100100 00100000 01101001 01101110 00001101
00001010 01000001 01101110 01100100 00100000 01101001 01110100
00100000 01110011 01101111 01110101 01101110 01100100 01100101
01100100 00100000 01110011 01101111 01101101 01100101 01110100
01101000 01101001 01101110 01100111 00100000 01101100 01101001

141

01101011 01100101 00100000 01110100 01101000 01101001 01110011
00001101 00001010

[Fiddle solo]

01010111 01101000 01100101 01101110 00100000 01110100 01101000
01100101 00100000 01100100 01100101 01110110 01101001 01101100
00100000 01100110 01101001 01101110 01101001 01110011 01101000
01100101 01100100 00001101 00001010 01001010 01101111 01101000
01101110 01101110 01111001 00100000 01110011 01100001 01101001
01100100 00100000 01110111 01100101 01101100 01101100 00100000
01111001 01101111 01110101 00100111 01110010 01100101 00100000
01110000 01110010 01100101 01110100 01110100 01111001 00100000
01100111 01101111 01101111 01100100 00100000 01101111 01101100
01100100 00100000 01110011 01101111 01101110 00001101 00001010
01001010 01110101 01110011 01110100 00100000 01110011 01101001
01110100 00100000 01110010 01101001 01100111 01101000 01110100
00100000 01101001 01101110 00100000 01110100 01101000 01100001
01110100 00100000 01100011 01101000 01100001 01101001 01110010
00100000 01110010 01101001 01100111 01101000 01110100 00100000
01110100 01101000 01100101 01110010 01100101 00001101 00001010
01000001 01101110 01100100 00100000 01101100 01100101 01110100
00100000 01101101 01100101 00100000 01110011 01101000 01101111
01110111 00100000 01111001 01101111 01110101 00100000 01101000
01101111 01110111 00100000 01101001 01110100 00100111 01110011
00100000 01100100 01101111 01101110 01100101 00001101 00001010

01001000 01100101 00100000 01110000 01101100 01100001 01111001
01100101 01100100 00100000 01000110 01101001 01110010 01100101
00100000 01101111 01101110 00100000 01110100 01101000 01100101
00100000 01001101 01101111 01110101 01101110 01110100 01100001
01101001 01101110 00001101 00001010 01010010 01110101 01101110
00100000 01100010 01101111 01111001 01110011 00101100 00100000
01110010 01110101 01101110 00001101 00001010 01010100 01101000
01100101 00100000 01100100 01100101 01110110 01101001 01101100
00100111 01110011 00100000 01101001 01101110 00100000 01110100
01101000 01100101 00100000 01001000 01101111 01110101 01110011
01100101 00100000 01101111 01100110 00100000 01110100 01101000
01100101 00100000 01010010 01101001 01110011 01101001 01101110
01100111 00100000 01010011 01110101 01101110 00001101 00001010
01000011 01101000 01101001 01100011 01101011 01100101 01101110
00100000 01101001 01101110 00100000 01100001 00100000 01100010
01110010 01100101 01100001 01100100 00100000 01110000 01100001
01101110 00100000 01110000 01101001 01100011 01101011 01100101
01101110 00100111 00100000 01101111 01110101 01110100 00100000
01100100 01101111 01110101 01110011 01100111 01101000 00001101 00001010
01000111 01110010 01100001 01101110 01101110 01111001 00100000
01100100 01101111 01100101 01110011 00100000 01111001 01101111

THE BINARY CODE TRANSLATION

01110101 01110010 00100000 01100100 01101111 01100111 00100000
01100010 01101001 01110100 01100101 00001101 00001010 01001110
01101111 00100000 01100011 01101000 01101001 01101100 01100100
00101100 00100000 01101110 01101111

[Fiddle solo]

01010100 01101000 01100101 00100000 01100100 01100101 01110110
01101001 01101100 00100000 01100010 01101111 01110111 01100101
01100100 00100000 01101000 01101001 01110011 00100000 01101000
01100101 01100001 01100100 00001101 00001010 01000010 01100101
01100011 01100001 01110101 01110011 01100101 00100000 01101000
01100101 00100000 01101011 01101110 01100101 01110111 00100000
01110100 01101000 01100001 01110100 00100000 01101000 01100101
00100111 01100100 00100000 01100010 01100101 01100101 01101110
00100000 01100010 01100101 01100001 01110100 00001101 00001010
01000001 01101110 01100100 00100000 01101000 01100101 00100000
01101100 01100001 01101001 01100100 00100000 01110100 01101000
01100001 01110100 00100000 01100111 01101111 01101100 01100100
01100101 01101110 00100000 01100110 01101001 01100100 01100100
01101100 01100101 00001101 00001010 01001111 01101110 00100000
01110100 01101000 01100101 00100000 01100111 01110010 01101111
01110101 01101110 01100100 00100000 01100001 01110100 00100000
01001010 01101111 01101000 01101110 01101110 01111001 00100111
01110011 00100000 01100110 01100101 01100101 01110100 00001101
00001010

01001010 01101111 01101000 01101110 01101110 01111001 00100000
01110011 01100001 01101001 01100100 00101100 00100000 01000100
01100101 01110110 01101001 01101100 00100000 01101010 01110101
01110011 01110100 00100000 01100011 01101111 01101101 01100101
00100000 01101111 01101110 00100000 01100010 01100001 01100011
01101011 00001101 00001010 01001001 01100110 00100000 01111001
01101111 01110101 00100000 01100101 01110110 01100101 01110010
00100000 01110111 01100001 01101110 01101110 01100001 00100000
01110100 01110010 01111001 00100000 01100001 01100111 01100001
01101001 01101110 00001101 00001010 01001001 00100000 01100100
01101111 01101110 01100101 00100000 01110100 01101111 01101100
01100100 00100000 01111001 01101111 01110101 00100000 01101111
01101110 01100011 01100101 00100000 01111001 01101111 01110101
00100000 01110011 01101111 01101110 00100000 01101111 01100110
00100000 01100001 00100000 01100010 01101001 01110100 01100011
01101000 00001101 00001010 01001001 00100111 01101101 00100000
01110100 01101000 01100101 00100000 01100010 01100101 01110011
01110100 00100000 01110100 01101000 01100101 01110010 01100101

00100111 01110011 00100000 01100101 01110110 01100101 01110010
00100000 01100010 01100101 01100101 01100101 0110111 00001101 00001010[85]

01000001 01101110 01100100 00100000 01101000 01100101 00100000
01110000 01101100 01100001 01111001 01100101 01100100 00100000
01000110 01101001 01110010 01100101 00100000 01101111 01101110
00100000 01110100 01101000 01100101 00100000 01001101 01101111
01110101 01101110 01110100 01100001 01101001 01101110 00001101
00001010 01010010 01110101 01101110 00100000 01100010 01101111
01111001 01110011 00101100 00100000 01110010 01110101 01101110
00001101 00001010 01010100 01101000 01100101 00100000 01100100
01100101 01110110 01101001 01101100 00100111 01110011 00100000
01101001 01101110 00100000 01110100 01101000 01100101 00100000
01001000 01101111 01110101 01110011 01100101 00100000 01101111
01100110 00100000 01110100 01101000 01100101 00100000 01010010
01101001 01110011 01101001 01101110 01100111 00100000 01010011
01110101 01101110 00001101 00001010 01000011 01101000 01101001
01100011 01101011 01100101 01101110 00100000 01101001 01101110
00100000 01100001 00100000 01100010 01110010 01100101 01100001
01100100 00100000 01110000 01100001 01101110 00100000 01110000
01101001 01100011 01101011 01100101 01101110 00100111 00100000
01101111 01110101 01110100 00100000 01100100 01101111 01110101
01100111 01101000 00001101 00001010 01000111 01110010 01100001
01101110 01101110 01111001 00100000 01100100 01101111 01100101
01110011 00100000 01111001 01101111 01110101 01110010 00100000
01100100 01101111 01100111 00100000 01100010 01101001 01110100
01100101 00001101 00001010 01001110 01101111 00100000 01100011
01101000 01101001 01101100 01100100 00101100 00100000 01101110
01101111 00001101 00001010

Words & music © The Charlie Daniels Band

Now that you know the truth, go forth and spread the word!

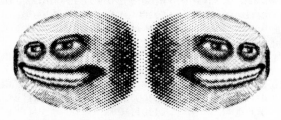

---

[85] 01010100 01101000 01100001 01110100 11100010 10000000
10011001 01110011 00100000 01010000 01101111 01110000 01100101
00100000 01000111 01110101 01110011 11100010 10000000 10011001
01110011 00100000 01100110 01100001 01110110 01101111 01110010
01101001 01110100 01100101 00100000 01110110 01100101 01110010
01110011 01100101 00101110

BY BEING, IT IS.

The Charlie Daniels Entity: Epistemologically dense
and hermeneutically multilayered, it is shown
here stripped of the *bourgeoisie* affectations of
comprehensibility and standard human form

APPENDIX X

THE
(RELATIVE) TRUTH
ABOUT QUING

CLASSIFIED: **Top Secret**
BISCUITEER INFORMATION
MEMORANDUM # 23.5
Rank c-17 and above only
Document 546.24, Operation Sausage-Asphalt
Directive S&B 322

INTELLIGENCE OPERATIVES IN CHARGE:
General Tso, Colonel Sanders and Captain Crunch

Warning: *For advanced initiates only, not to be shared with outsiders*

Quing is a way of life. Quing is a belief-system that does not believe in believing, but don't believe it. Worship all others before Quing, but don't think about it. God-Biscuit: No chin, no legs.

• Quing is all things except that which is Quing. Quing is not unlike Quing on a cross, on a rope, in a can. Do not think about Quing, but don't think about it.

• The only way not to know about Quing with definite uncertainty is to unlearn all the things you don't know about Quing, but don't think about it. To visualize Quing you must imagine everything that is not Quing; that is precisely what Quing looks like. Sit up all night not thinking about Quing. God-Biscuit: No chin, no legs.

• Quing is like all the thoughts you've never thought of, but don't think about it. Quing is not unlike all of the time not spent during fishing trips you've never taken. Contemplate Quing by not thinking of Quing.

• Quing is like a life form without the qualities generally attributed to life forms. Quing is not unlike a form of furry golfballs, but don't think about it. Do not think about Quing and you will be the foremost disciple of Quing. God-Biscuit: No chin, no legs.

• Do not allow Quing not to be small animals risking gastric distress. Quing can neither confirm nor deny that Quing is or is not an alcoholic without a mouth falling off a double-decker bus in slow motion. Win a date with Quing; entries must not be submitted.

• Do not refrain from not talking about Quing with all of the people you wish you knew. Quing is like cold fire, but don't think about it. Quing may or may not be larger and smaller than the period at the end of this sentence. God-Biscuit: No chin, no legs.

• Don't live out your wildest fantasies with Quing. Learn how to be Quing by not being Quing. Quing can only harm you if you think about Quing, but don't think about it.

• Do not live like those who would not live unlike Quing. Quing is a surrogate dreamer for a world without dreams. Sing along with Quing as Quing sings Quingself. God-Biscuit: No chin, no legs.

• Do not define definitions with Quing. Do not reconsider Quing. Quing in flight; don't think about it.

• Quing-box without surfaces. Preach Quing but don't think about it. Dehydrated Quing deprivation. God-Biscuit: No chin, no legs.

• Add a twist of Quing to your evening. Thinking about Quing is like not thinking about Quing, but don't think about not thinking about it. Quing is only and always what Quing is and/or is not.

• Teenage dreams of Quing. Do not tell your children about Quing and they will not love Quing even less. Do not put Quing on your toothbrush. God-Biscuit: No chin, no legs.

• Do not listen to the confessions of Quing. You have been led not to disbelieve Quing, but don't believe it. Fan the flames of Quing and then get out of the way.

• Quing is everything in the universe except Quing, but don't think about it. Quing envy. You have been told repeatedly not to think about Quing, but don't think about it. God-Biscuit: No chin, no legs.

• Do not allow Quing to operate heavy farm machinery while Quing is not animals or small children. That which is not Quing has been known to remind humans of that which is not Quing. Do not check your hair for Quing.

• Pay no attention to the words that Quing does not speak. Do not think about Quing while under the influence of Quing. Quing is the lack thereof. God-Biscuit: No chin, no legs.

• Quing is every step you have never taken. Quing is potentially a potential enigma. Do not allow Quing not to happen to your family.

• Do not be fooled by imitation Quing. If it is not Quing it is Quing. If it is Quing it is not Quing. God-Biscuit: No chin, no legs.

• Quing is smaller than the universe, which is smaller than Quing. Quing country does not consist of Quing. Quing defines Quingself by actively not being Quing.

• Quing is not unlike a 1.5-wheeled tricycle, a one-sided icosahedron, or a three-legged biped, but don't think about it. Love Quing, eat Quing, experience Quing, ponder Quing, be Quing, but don't think about Quing. Quing does not eat your food. God-Biscuit: No chin, no legs.

—Excerpted from *Confessions of a Teenage Quing-Fiend* by Pope Gus Rasputin Nishnabotna Sni-A-Bar Freak the First and Rev. Zum Splurb. Published by Epileptic Aardvark Publications, 1753.

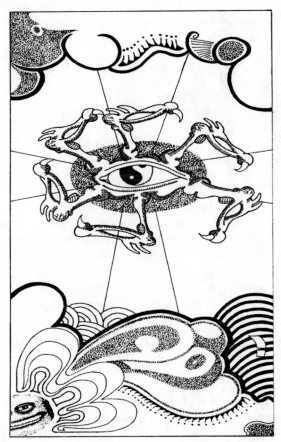

"To know exactly where you are you have to know exactly where you're not."

—Leroy "Wicker" Lincoln
Keynote Speaker, Zenarchist Symposium:
Am Good Grammer Are Counter-Revolutionary?

APPENDIX XI

THE HOLY BOOKS OF THE BISCUITIST CANON

Hey fellers!!!
Don't forget to nag your folks for these great Biscuitist publications!

They're the *ginchiest!!!*

Sarsaparilla Gorilla: Loaded 'n Cocked

Sarsaparilla Gorilla roams the saloons and soda fountains of the 1870s Wild West, seeking out friendly hombres to buy him beverages to cure the raging venereal diseases he caught from a time-traveling clam. Savor the wacky narrative complications that arise from interspecies communication breakdowns as our hirsute hero, heavily armed and with a twitchy, syphilitic trigger finger, sits there thirsty and dripping, oozing pus and frustration, becoming more itchy and agitated with each misunderstood plea for refreshments!

"ENJOY SYPHILLIS" WITH SARSAPARILLA GORILLA IN LOADED 'N COCKED

The Passionately Casual Mueslix Deliveryman

This morality play chronicles the adventures of Meretricious Maynard, fresh from the pages of "Mesodermic Messianic Mergansers." Struggling to save his family of woodchucks from the brothers Dinglebury and Dookie D. Duck, those ravenous flesh-eating mallards that thrive on the pain of root canal fetishists, Maynard has arrived in the nick of time with a well-endowed stash of mueslix.

Behold: Zwieback!

The Cracker is back! Thrill to this graphic depiction of bread-leavening ceremonies and dulcimer playing in the hidden outer space refuge of the Huguenauts! Parents will appreciate the subtext that, even on the distant fringe of the solar system, 'tis still crucial to realize that twerps have feelings too!

This logo is for the upcoming soap opera, based on the book!

Star Trek 3.141592: The Search for Hank Williams

A Braille adaptation of an interpretive dance! Nonplussed, Spock yodels, gurgles and burgles the cuds of an erstwhile gaggle of *vicuñae*. Honky the Albino Penguin finally groks the equinoctial precession with the aid of Minnie Pearl's victualler. Plus: Events take a turn to the dark side when Klingons unleash the dreaded proctonauts to probe Uranus!

Exciting Tales of Stimulating Inflammation
Trundling through the mall in a desperate attempt to gain freedom from Oinkster 2Rock the Unambiguously Gender-Neutral and Narcoleptically Somnambulistic Porcine Hip-Hop Hypnotherapist, Gertie's thong chafes her enormous, swaying egg sac.

The Jittery Barnacle Does It Again

The Jittery Barnacle Does It Again
Doctor Dudley Dean's dactylic hexadecimal speech patterns continue to annoy his patients. Plus: A game theory experiment goes horribly awry as the pustule ruptures!

Feverishly Apprehensive Yarns of Mirth
Scrappy and Schweitzer battle Toader Bubuoig for control of eighth century Poland! Plus bonus backup feature: It's the California Raisins vs. the Fruit of the Loom mascots, in a ferocious and fibrous replay of Caesar's battle against the Cisalpine Gauls after crossing the Rubicon in 49 B.C.!

Name That Tuna: The Lacunatics of Laguna Beach
A concise tragicomic primer on the aberrant zenarchist philosophies of the nation's most notorious serial mattress-tag remover, Leroy "Wicker" Lincoln. Such a hardcore anarchist that he refuses even to obey basic traffic signals, "Wicker" runs a red light and gets crushed beneath the wheels of a classified military tanker truck loaded down with a flotilla of liquefied tactical assault mammals!

The New Adventures of Pugnaciously Prognathous Man
Equally equipped with big jaws and a bad attitude, learn the prognosis of progressively prognathous Biff as he yearns to control the hairy wart-like swellings of his heritage.

Yankin' Tales of Protuberances

Infested with lice, Yorick's alien implant malfunctions as he alternates wildly between compulsive masturbation and sending prank-call smoke signals to Charles Q. Cheese, the pizza-dispensing rodent.

CHiPs: Pulse-Pounding Tales of Solipsism

Skeeter and Blodgett are much more than just motorcycle cops, they're conjoined twins! Joined at the back, one is deaf, the other is blind, and both are mute. Zen hilarity ensues when, armed with little more than their severely skewed sense of subjectivity, they attempt to stop the Exacerbative Weasel from smuggling almost 784,000,895 hagfish into Drop City!

Quibbles of the Damned: Rage of the Omega-Munchkin

It's everyone's favorite cattle-wrasslin' cowpoke, good ol' Filbert 'Fecal-Eye' McGee vs. the Honky-Tonk Troglodyte, in "And Lo!, Men Call Him... 'Troglodyte'"! Bonus pin-up: A dodecahedron with 12 nipples!

Stroke My Zither *(80 Page Giant)*

The story you dared us to tell! "Which Be Mightier, the Zither or the Bassoon?!?"

Intriguing Metanarratives Involving the Lizard with Excess Cartilage
Everyone's favorite dial-a-lizard demands vengeance in the plankton version of Heaven!

Suspenseful Punjabi Dentistry
Plumply Polypped Pudgett plops atop the gubernatorial campaign of Gumbo the Magnificent. Meanwhile, Vergil's gusset bursts, exposing Thrasymachus's shaven armpits to the ever-attenuating vernacular glance of the passing masses.

Fables of Mutants With and/or Without Palates
Ululatin' Ulysses lets loose a strained, meaty gurgle in his ubiquitous mucilaginity.

Tuber! *(One-shot)*
Afloat in his umiak on the open seas, will Tuber!, the Potato of Providence extirpate his need to provide extreme unction after Aunt May's topiary freakout?

For Whom Does That Porridge Undulate?
After a long day of quoin-wrasslin' the last thing a *faux* faun wants to do is commit a *faux pas*.

Tales of Guano
Guano, that lovably mobile, itinerant heap of semi-sentient mallard feces, struggles to acclimate to a worn-out elastic waistband as he starts life anew out yonder on the Martian bayou! Collectors' edition scratch 'n' sniff cover!

ALL HAIL THE LORD OF DOUGH!

Three cups of yeast for the Biscuits Ped will make,
Seven for "Wicker" and His ovens of stone,
Nine cups to mix *real* Biscuits, not fake,
One for the God-Biscuit upon Hir Doughy Throne,
In the stoves of Heaven, where the Biscuits bake.
One Dough to knead the souls, one Dough to bake them,
One Dough to give them life and better people make them
In the stoves of Heaven, where the Biscuits bake.

APPENDIX XII

A *COSMOGIRL!* PROFILE OF THE GOD-BISCUIT

(Reprinted with permission from the November 8, 1640 issue of CosmoGirl! *magazine. Interview conducted via email by Anne Hutchinson.)*

Dig it, baby! It's the Divine Deity of Dough! **So, Divine G-B, tell us about Yourself! What are You wearing?**

A: *Guten tag*, darling! I'm wearing *Oscar de la Renta* overalls with 200 tiny little zippered pockets sewn in, and each pocket carries an acorn to symbolize acornity; I finish off this ensemble with a pterodactyl-foreskin cummerbund from *Paul Smith*, psychedelic iridescent leather wingtips from *London Underground*, and a *Bulgari* portable scaffold built onto My shoulders, from which dangles a sword as I perform an interpretive dance routine called 'The Letter Opener of Damocles' for My peeps at the local lint mill. My lilac eyeliner is from *Revlon*, plaid lip gloss from *Maybelline*, the wax on My handlebar mustache is from *Kiehl's*, My breast implants are by *Tupperware*, My cornrows were braided by *Suubi's* in North Hollywood, My G-string is from *Victoria's Secret*, parasol from *Lord & Taylor*, do-rag from *Stazzon*, and the lens of My monocle was precision-ground and polished by Galileo Galilei himself.

Q: What is Your first or most cherished memory?

A: OMG, My first and only cherished memory has to do with having a hair pulled. When I proposed Myself into being at the dawn of the universe I was a fairly typical primordially-powerful cosmic baby, but I had a single very long hair that grew out of the small of My back. It was black and greasy and about fourteen inches long when I was "born". For whatever reason I never thought to cut it or tweeze it or anything, so by the time I was three I had this one oily hair that straggled from My back and was about fifty furlongs in length; when I roamed around the castle it would drag behind Me and get snagged up in the household pets. One day immediately prior to puberty, I escaped from Griselda[86], jumped out of the incubator and ran naked out the back door into the yard. My long, billowing follicle got entangled on the baroque welding of the cast iron lawn chair and was yanked out, roots and all. 'Twas, like, totally tormentous.

<u>Ah, the carefree days of childhood</u>: Two of God-Biscuit's favorite photos from Hir youth, taken at summer camp after snorkeling betwixt the light beams behind Quing's meat stall.

Q: What do You look like?
A: My height fluctuates wildly, ranging between roughly 1.6180339887498948482045 micrometers to 498.1 parsecs, depending on the pull of the lunar tides at any given moment. In addition to wreaking havoc on My wardrobe, this effect can be somewhat disorienting to others: My body contour pulses and shimmers, advancing and receding like a crazed octopus without arms gesticulating wildly in one of those *OBJECTS IN MIRROR ARE CLOSER THAN THEY APPEAR* rear-view mirrors. The surface of My exoskeleton is a very low-viscosity hyperdimensional fluid-based fractal, flowing and

---

[86] The nanny.

dripping in constant motion like maple syrup drizzled over a cantaloupe. When I so choose I can grow as many as eleven arms like an asymmetrical Hindu statue; each arm ends in a puffy white four-fingered glove, smoothing the edge off of My intimidating appearance with its friendly and nostalgic Mickey Mouse connotation. My pheromones are so turbo-charged they emit little revving sounds as they squirt out of My glands in asynchronous bursts of liquid static. Worshippers often have trouble seeing Me through My arcing pleochroic halo of sparking synaptic firings and Hawking radiation as I hover above the pulpits and parapets of Arglebargle the AbodeBiscuit, thrashing them lovingly from within the confines of My own gravity well.

Q: What famous people do You most resemble?
A: I look like a cross between the character Fish from *Barney Miller*, a topologically warped and slightly squashed beige *Gobstopper*, Joe Pesci, Jane Leeves and the tyrannosaurus rex from the 1981 Ringo Starr movie *Caveman*, if all of these personae were wetware-processed into biochip format and coalesced into a silicon-gel vacuum-sealed foil-stamped die-cut precision-molded *Jean-Paul Gaultier* steam-powered cyborg body. Imagine a corpulently spherical R2-D2 with mutton-chop sideburns, a comb-over and a doughy hair-covered prosthetic proboscis that sticks out of his back, and that's Me.

Q: When is Your favorite time of day?
A: I prefer to drag My non-orientable, ectoplasmic, perfluoro-octanoic acid-coated, red-shifted and wildly-Dopplering Brobdingnagian bulk through the humid, muck-encrusted streets of pre-dawn ArglebargleOpolis, thinking about life while My eyes squeeze out little droplets of ammonia-laden pus, the unfortunate byproduct of a gene-spliced metabolism run rampant.[87] Being quite evanescent

---

[87] I have recently crossbred Myself with a gene-modified tomato fitted with the digestive tract of a bandicoot; My metabolic byproducts are particularly lethal at the moment as My body struggles to reach homeostasis.

and lighter than air, My metabolic effluvia rapidly diffuse into My surroundings, permeating the environment and choking bystanders, covering them with the hydrochloric byproducts of My passing. Under stressful conditions I have been known to secrete mucilaginous paste from My pores in one rapid squelch, like a million microscopic tubes of toothpaste all being squeezed at once from somewhere deep inside. So the emptier the streets, the better.

'Tis burdensome to be a God.

Q: What is Your favorite prime number?
A: 104,729. I'm just sayin'.

Q: What color are Your eyes?
A: My eyes are puce in color, but instead of standard mammalian eyelids, Mine are quite different. Rather than an ocular cavity with a flap-like lid that closes over the eyeball and keeps it moist, I must repeatedly resort to two methods of eyeball moisturization: I can either uncoil My warty six foot tongue from its containment module to lick the eyeball like some wimpy tree sloth, or I can use My pneumatic hook to extract a bottle of *Chanel No. 5* from My utility belt. A spritz or two in the morning keeps Me fresh all day!

Rather than embedded eye-sockets I have bilaterally placed eyes on short stalks at both sides of My chitinous and cartilaginous head. These wall-eyed stalks are hooked into My turbo-charged and picotechnologically-enhanced nervous system to scrunch up into little rings to protect My infrared-capable bulging peepers, which were quite expensive to have custom designed. They can look a bit out of place wobbling around and quivering excitedly from the sides of My face, but after I had them tattooed with blue eyeliner they are much less noticeable. LOL

Q: What are You most proud of that few people know about You?
A: If I eat a bushel of communion wafers I can navigate through the darkness of the primordially-chaotic pre-Creation

void by means of high-pitched echolocation bursts from My hypersonic infrasound stomach gurgles.[88]

Q: What aspect of Yourself would You most like to work on?
A: I am, by definition, *infallible*. That said, however, I must admit that occasionally I fly into homicidal Old Testament-style raging temper tantrums and would like to kill the killer who kills all who don't kill themselves.

Q: All right readers, that's all for now. Thanks again for creating the universe, Big G-B!
A: My pleasure Anne! Let's do lunch sometime. Have your people call My people. And BTW: A big shout-out to My homie, DJ G-zuss! BFF!

MORE COSMOGIRL! *FUN FACTS ABOUT* *THE GOD-BISCUIT:*

Favorite musicians: *The Whom*, the world's most objective rock band.

Favorite past-time: Hiding out in deep underground bunkers and corrupting gaggles of Ediacaran swamp flounders.

Favorite Holiday Song: *We Wish You A Happy Platypusmas*[89]

Fashion tip: "Clothes make the mammal."

Day job: Supreme Being of the Universe, Almighty Lord and Ruler of Creation, &c.

Night jobs: *Saturday-Tuesday*: Proletarian rabble-rouser at a Metamucil factory
Wednesday-Friday: Silkscreening the word "Sunkist" onto all them oranges

---

[88] Please refer to footnote 22.
[89] *Platypusmas*: A celebration of the resurrection of Leroy "Wicker" Lincoln. If "Wicker" sees His shadow after rising from the dead, that means there's still six more weeks of winter.

God-Biscuit's pet peeves (in ascending order):

1. The third-degree burns that result from the gravy that flows forth from My nasal septum.

2. The monkey's finger only *looks* stiff.

3. The dance contest was cancelled after their skin peeled off.

4. The otter's undulations aren't indicative of anything; in the end they fail to signify.

5. When I said "bottlenose" I really meant it!

6. Time will be around for a long time, and for a long time after that.

7. Even Albino Darth has to admit that the idea of a hunter-seeker killer robot retrofitted with the floppy jowls and droopy eyes of a basset hound is ridiculous.

8. The baby elephant convulses wildly after Jumbolina Jolie hacks off its trunk with an axe.

9. Time flies during subjective perception of frivolity and/or zygomatic flexure-inducing interactive experiential matrices.

When God-Biscuit is overwhelmed by the itch to be iterative, God-Biscuit proposes God-Biscuit.

APPENDIX XIII

MEDITATIONS ON THE 24 DIMENSIONS OF THE GOD-BISCUIT

EVERYTHING YOU NEED TO KNOW ABOUT REALITY, IN CONVENIENT *HAIKU* FORM!

Encoded with sub-subliminal mnemonic trigger words for maximized retinal retention, synaptic absorption & dendritic distribution

The God-Biscuit smites
the SpapOopGannopOlop,
stopping evil's reign

Bandicoots rotate
in supernova sunshine.
Hairless! Imploding!

'Twas the largest mass
of molten cheese ever known
to coagulate

Monkey and eggplant,
mating ritual gone wrong:
human race is born

Mighty flippers flail,
"The Nuclear Platypus!"
Unbelievers wail

Biscuit believers,
a goal toward which to strive:
Biscuitoid Mutant

Night: To you I come
with buckets of melted cheese
and no chin, no legs

Arglebargle Church
The only church that matters
Biscuit Cult Supreme

One-sided pancake
nourishes the hungry soul,
prevents paperclips

**Biscuit of Judgment:
Yeast Beast of Apocalypse,
Varmint of Vengeance**

**I say unto you
it is not necessary
to read this haiku**

**Transcendental Dough:
For whom does the Biscuit bake?
Lo!, it bakes for thee**

Bill of Rights should say,
"E Pluribus Biscuitus"
Alas, it does not

"This sentence is false."
"Cheeseplug: don't think about it."
Words by which to live

"Do fish like *Cheez Whiz*?"
A question to contemplate
while yodeling hymns

Flaming tree sloth with
no eyelids, seeks your help to
keep his eyeballs moist

Behold, BisQuitus:
the end of reality
already happened

"All hail the dreaded
Corpulent Bondage Frog,"
so say the lost souls

Pope Gus once ate a
black market unicorndog.
The next day: *regret*

With Flour Power
the Majestic Monotreme
helps you flex your spleen

Always remember:
Ped Xing baked for your sins,
and it really hurt

Dough or die; so says
Shaved bear, talking lemon.
Sounds like good advice

God-Biscuit = "Not real"
Anti-Doughist fallacy,
a blasphemer's creed

Behold: in the end
the love you take is equal
to the Dough you bake

APPENDIX XIV

RIGOROUS AND LOGIC-BASED PROOF THAT DEATH DOES NOT EXIST

THE FUDDITE TRANSLATION

<u>Note</u>: *After God-Biscuit's traumatic early experiences with speech impediments,* (see *Biscuitus,* verses 14-16 for more info) *we humbly present to the reader the following translation of Appendix XIV, in solidarity with our brothers and sisters afflicted with Fuddism.*

People often speak of theiw fiwst memowy, pewhaps a chewished moment fwom theiw eawly childhood. The concept of a *fiwst memowy*, of couwse, cawwies with it the welative existence of a *last memowy* as well, fow thewe can be no "fiwst" without a "last" and so on. As the fiwst memowy occuws in childhood, the last memowy would occuw immediately pwiow to death.

But how does the mechanism of a "last memowy" opewate? To have a memowy of something means thewe must be a pewiod of awaweness *aftew* the event wemembewed, a duwation duwing which the wemembewew has time to fowm a memowy of the event that just occuwwed. Duwing such a pewiod of memowy fowmation, howevew, one would also be in the midst of new expewiences that would be memowable in and of themselves.

So thewe is, in fact, no possibility fow such a thing as a "last memowy." Like Zeno's dichotomy pawadox, which says that in owdew to go fwom point A to point B one must fiwst twavel half that distance, but fiwst has to twavel halfway to the halfway point, but fiwst halfway to the halfway of the halfway point, *ad infinitum,* a last memowy could only be fowmed *aftew* the event wemembewed, and duwing that intewval yet anothew last memowy would fowm, and while that was being encoded in memowy yet anothew memowy would fowm, and so on in an infinite wegwess.

Even if the incoming sensowy input of the wemembewew wewe shut down thewe would still be memowies of the immediately pwevious memowy fowmation, and then a subsequent memowy of the memowy of memowy fowmation &c. So if thewe is no such thing as a last memowy it follows that thewe is no such thing as a final end-point bit of awaweness, which means that we now no longew have any excuse to die. When people "die" and see the white light they awe actually seeing *The Gweat White Light of the Oven on High,* bwight and wadiant as they entew the oven to be baked into theiw next incawnation.

So hewe, at last, is wigowous and logic-based pwoof[90] that consciousness will nevew die. *Wejoice, Biscuiteew! Thewe is no death!*

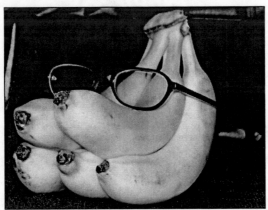

**The threat of potential SpapOopGannopOlopianism
requires eternal vigilance.**
(Current Homeland Security Color-Coded Threat Level = Plaid)

---

[90] Based on a favored sophistic principle known by Biscuitists as *Occam's Tweezer,* the "Law of Selectivity" by which one plucks/selects only the specific ideas and facts that help make one's case appear to be true, or at the very least vaguely logical.

APPENDIX XV

GOD-BISCUIT'S INSTRUCTIONS TO YOU, *THE FAITHFUL*

I

The words and images you have just experienced were specially formulated by Arglebargle Reality-Technicians to rearrange the neurons of your brain. As you read this, all brain cells unnecessary to your functioning as a Biscuitoid Mutant are blinking out of existence, fizzing and popping in tiny neuroelectrical bursts. Your remaining neuron-clusters are being bombarded with gigapixel Flour Power ontology-graft downloads never experienced by *mere humans* who have yet to encounter *The Nuclear Platypus Biscuit Bible*.

Even if you are only browsing this book and just happened to skim this very paragraph, it is most likely too late: simply coming into contact with The Nuclear Platypus Biscuit Bible has plugged you directly into the **Arglebargle Reality-Nullification Field**. Even now members of the *Cosmic Coincidence Control Center* are filing the paperwork required to process your claim, so prepare posthaste for a visit from the infamous *Men in Plaid*, bearing their dreaded Stealth Onion That Is Impervious To Radar Detection. By now the Doughy Love of the God-Biscuit has penetrated the interstitial spaces between the atoms of your body, saturating and bonding with every molecular surface, unclogging your mind canals and radically expanding your reality tunnels with the dogma-destroying power of **Plausible Defiability**.[91] [92]

Now that your very brain and DNA code have been restructured by the White Hot Word of the God-Biscuit, you possess knowledge that has been denied to the masses of humanity for millennia. You can now truthfully say to non-Biscuiteers, "You may be strange, but I'm *mutated.*"

While the profound power and glory of Biscuitism can indeed be intoxicating, with great power comes great responsibility. *Biscuithood is a position of incredible power and is not to be taken lightly.*

II

[APPENDIX XV, SUBSECTION II, DETAILING ALL KNOWN EMERGENCY CONTAINMENT PROCEDURES IN THE EVENT OF AN UNANNOUNCED ONTOLOGY INCURSION BY GOD-BISCUIT'S SKANKY, FISHY-SMELLING FORMER REHAB ROOMMATE, *COD-BISCUIT*, HAS BEEN REDACTED FOR SECURITY REASONS. THIS SUBSECTION WILL BE DECLASSIFIED AND REINSERTED IN THIS SPACE ONCE THE PUBLIC HAS BEEN DEEMED READY TO RECEIVE SUCH ADVANCED OCCULT INFORMATION.]

III

As a Biscuiteer it is imperative that you *obey no commands*, including this one. The Biscuiteer is a law unto

---

[91] The weapon of choice of Militant Agnostics everywhere.

[92] As an added incentive, you are now eligible to redeem *Bonus Biscuit Points* by using **The Blessed God-Biscuit Emoticon**: (:l)

hirself, autonomous of all authority other than hir own. **There are no limits.** (Some restrictions may apply.)

However, there is one area in which the Biscuiteer must feel compelled to act: The consumption of amazingly large amounts of caffeine. Caffeine is the ultimate weapon of the SpapOopGannopOlop. As is shown in *The Gospel of the Nuclear Platypus*, verse 33, it is the SpapOopGannopOlop's fearsome plan to transform all of the universe's hydrogen into caffeine, completely hypercaffeinating and wiring the universe until, mega-jittery, it vibrates itself out of existence.

The only way to survive this imminent *Caffeinated Universal Vibratory Annihilation* is to consume as much caffeine as possible, thereby building up a tolerance and immunity to the universal caffeination.

Any substance that does not contain caffeine is a weapon of the SpapOopGannopOlop designed to keep us vulnerable. In the interest of self-preservation it is suggested that all Biscuiteers avoid all caffeine-free substances so as to leave room within oneself for large quantities of caffeine.

Any time you feel the need for guidance, simply ask yourself, "WTFWG-BD?"

IV

Highly skilled **Arglebargle Actuality Nullification Specialists** have scientifically verified and refined the apocalyptic claims of the Holy Chapter of *BisQuitus*, and the results are glorious and terrifying to behold! **Civilization and reality itself will indeed cease to exist within 72 hours of the exact moment that *YOU* read *these three words*.** Infallible Biscuitist prophets have declared that the absolute probability of this happening has been verified with **100% certainty** to be most likely 99.99999797% possible.[93]

As was pointed out, the universe came to an end a long time ago, but so far the vast consensus of observation-capable organisms within the universe has yet to take notice of this fact. However, within 72 hours of your reading this page the universe *will* notice, for *YOU* are the trigger, *the*

---

[93] With a margin of error of +/- 97.4%

catalyst itself, for the **Apocalyptic Universal Realization of the State of Universelessness**! It's all *your* fault!

Have no fear, however, and be not burdened by this fact. The aforementioned Arglebargle Actuality Nullification Specialists have teamed up alongside **Arglebargle Reality Technicians** to develop a way to save the universe from your reckless reading habits: The only way to save the universe is to destroy It before It destroys Itself!

This is the plan: Self-Directed Evolutionary Mutation Specialists have spread out around the planet, proselytizing and recruiting new Church members. At the current rate of membership growth, by noontime next Thursday 82% of the planetary population will have become Biscuitoid Mutants, at which point we will control an estimated 93.651% of the wealth and resources of the solar system.

Once this threshold is reached we will initiate *The Golden Path to Unlimited Universal Biscuitoid Salvation: The Vast Biscuitization of the Masses.* Atop hilltops and in remote forest bunkers and everywhere between, the Biscuitoid masses will join hand and hook, paw and claw to become one with the God-Biscuit, encasing Us/Them/It/Hirself in a self-recursive energy shell with no ties or relation to anything outside itself: We/They/It/S/He will thence be totally self-referential.

As this energy-Biscuit refers to Itself It will become more powerful, causing it to refer to Itself again with enhanced clarity and increased resolution, beginning the cycle anew and so on in what Paracelsus called an I.S.B.C.F.L.[94] This expanding system will become the long-prophesied **Infinitely Recursive TransUniversal Nullifier**, destroying not only the present universe, but also rippling back to destroy everything that ever existed in the past, all the way back to the moments prior to Creation, preventing the God-Biscuit Hirself and everything else from ever existing in the first place!

This *Biscuitoid Cosmocide* may sound like a particularly egregious case of nihilistically bad manners, but

---

[94] **I**nfinitely **S**olipsistic **B**iscuitoid **C**osmic **F**eedback **L**oop

it is our only hope. Once the universe is nipped in the bud it will be impossible for the BisQuit to occur, thus saving the universe: By preemptively destroying reality *the destruction of reality is itself destroyed*, allowing the universe to continue to exist! The cycle will be self-perpetuating and will continue indefinitely, because high-energy studies conducted at your town's local Arglebargle Particle Accelerator/Super-Collider Complex indicate that the universe can only exist if it doesn't exist, and can't not exist if it doesn't not lack nonexistence, and vice versa.

This will take some getting used to, but imagine how exciting life will be when the entire universe is destroyed and recreated an infinite number of times every nanosecond for all Eternity!

**Melvin-Marie "the Pruner" Snufflethwaite IV,
God-Biscuit's erstwhile stunt double.**

V

Literally thousands of groups based on planet Earth falsely claim to have been the first Biscuit religion, but only the Church of Arglebargle can rightfully boast of being **The World's Oldest and Largest Biscuit Cult.**

The imminent **Worldwide Biscuitist Hegemony** will be but the first stepping-stone toward irrevocable galactic conquest. The Biscuitoid masses will march forth from Earth, proudly brandishing the banners of the Glorious God-Biscuit as the Doughist Doctrine spreads to the shores of all lands and to the gravity wells of every planet and galactic cluster across all frequency domains of the omniverse. *Aye, and you, the Chosen Ones, will be at the very forefront of this most profound of all transformations!*

If you need Doughist guidance as you start to live a Biscuitist, or at least *Biscuitish*, lifestyle, please feel free to call our *Certified Biscuitoid Mutation Specialists* 365 hours a day, 24 days a week at (555) BISCUIT [(555) 867-5309].[95]

You can also commune with the glorious God-Biscuit online. The *Divine Website* contains updates, images, Church membership/ordainment info, Bible Study groups, ordering information for exclusive *Arglebargle Mutant Merchandise* such as t-shirts, hats, coffee mugs &c., and more:

http://www.god-biscuit.com

or, if you feel a need to pray to God-Biscuit, 'twould behoove you to do so by sending your prayers to the *Blessed Email*:

nuclear.platypus@god-biscuit.com

(Due to the incredible call volume of prayers, pleas, entreaties, appeals, recipe requests, beseechments, paternity/maternity lawsuits, imprecations, invocations, non-stick cooking spray recommendations, compliments, complaints, implorations, Biscuitoid benedictions, supplications, and lucrative sports merchandise endorsement offers that God-Biscuit receives every nanosecond, S/He is not always able to answer every prayer, though S/He will try Hir best. Rest assured that your Doughist Devotion is most appreciated, and that *God-Biscuit luvs thee*.)

IT IS TOO LATE TO GO BACK: God-Biscuit made you weird for a purpose, so indulge your abnormality. Enjoy your mutation, embrace your strangeness, and use your newfound powers wisely. Praise be unto the glory of the God-Biscuit!

---

[95] To save money we have recently outsourced our *Help Desk and Telemarketing Division* to remote areas of extremely unstable Third World countries. If you get the message, "Your call is very important to us. Our operators are currently busy helping other callers and/or fighting off leftist rebels, neocon theofascist death squads, imperialist petrodollar mercenaries, insurgent gun runners and/or narcoterrorist groups and are currently unable to take your call," then please be patient and don't call back later.

WARNING: Upon being accepted for membership to the Nuclear Platypus Church of Arglebargle you will have a strong feeling of *doughja-vu*, the overwhelming sense that you've seen that specific Biscuit before. Afterward, in addition to receiving your free commemorative Arglebargle toothpick holder, you will be blindfolded, thrown into an unmarked black van and taken for processing at the fenced-in complex of **Arglebargle Reeducation Camps,** charmingly renovated former CIA black site compounds in the remote forests of Eastern Europe. Upon completion of your doctrinal training your DNA code will project out of your eyelids on sideways light beams, crawling down your throat and flowing into your nostrils, ear canals, eye sockets and other major bodily orifices. This is a vital and necessary component of the Biscuitoid Mutation process, so do not be alarmed.

(Potential side effects may include constipation; drippy, bleeding eyes; unauthorized udders; and random bouts of spontaneous decapitation, in which last case you are hereby authorized to panic as you deem fit according to the customs of your people.)

Yea, the Future Looks Bright Indeed: Lo! A glorious new generation hearkens unto the clarion call of Biscuitism, boldly carrying the Flour Power of the God-Biscuit into a magnificent future heretofore undreamt. Yea, while the meek may inherit the Earth, the Bold and the Biscuitoid shall inherit the *stars.*

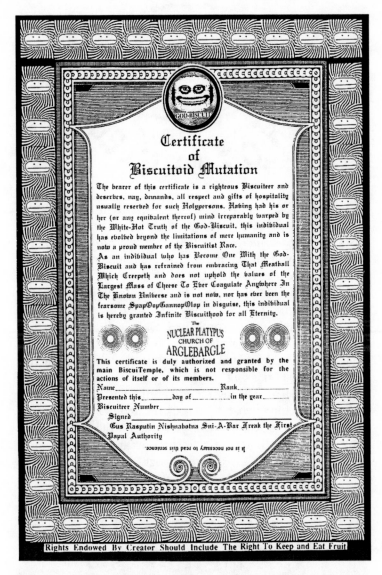

Oh what a glorious day 'twill be when the Ultimate Honor is bestowed upon thee, if indeed thou dost be found worthy! A privilege forever denied *mere humans*, you will realize your higher calling as a veritable Biscuitoid Mutant on the blessed morn you awake to find the above certificate eidetically tattooed onto the inner lining of your eyelids.

DISCLAIMER: A proven axiom of quantum physics states that any object is automatically altered when an outside force observes it. *The Nuclear Platypus Biscuit Bible*, alas, is no exception. If you didn't like this titanic tome don't blame us; *you're* the one who looked at it!

When this book left the printers it was called *A Curious Conniption Amidst the Corn Rows*. A feel-good tale of two adorable, newly-orphaned Okie children and their delightful canine companion Mr. Tootles, it followed their exploits in life, love and book-learnin' as they sought out their long-lost missing triplet in the rough 'n tumble vineyards of 1930s Depression-era northern California.

No telling what this book is about *now*, however, since *you* keep looking at it. If you weren't pleased with this book then please purchase a fresh copy and *read it without looking at it* and see if it's more to your liking.

ABOUT THE AUTHOR

Pope Gus Rasputin Nishnabotna Sni-A-Bar Freak the First,
shown here broadcasting the Blessed Biweekly BiscuiTelethon,
a pay-per-view plea for donations, from the rumpus room
of his secret bunker beneath the Bermuda Triangle.

Firstly, **Pope Gus Rasputin Nishnabotna Sni-A-Bar Freak the First**, *FreeBiscuit Extraordinaire*, is not his real name. His real name is a 24-dimensional vibration algorithmically encoded into the supersymmetrical sub-quantum infrastructure of "space/time" itself, with no beginning and no end, that is neither pronounceable nor even conceivable within the semiotic/conceptual/epistemological/ ontological/phenomenological limitations inherent to three-dimensional biophysically-manifest organisms composed of baryonic matter.

Regardless, he whom we know as Pope Gus[96] is one of the most important religious prophets ever to grace the soil of this or any other planet, and he has led a very mysterious life so far. Many rumors claim that he is actually a single-celled self-replicating amoeba-like organism, but these

---

[96] Or, as he's known in the hip-hop world, **Tha Massive G-Pope**.

pernicious and undoctrinal rumors were finally proven false when a team of paparazzi verified that Pope Gus is indeed visible without the aid of a microscope.

Having been born at a very early age in 1769 in Aemona, and blessed with a feral-yet-mellow disposition due to his being raised in the wild by cucumbers, Gus Rasputin Nishnabotna Sni-A-Bar Freak has long felt a sense of unity with Biscuits. When he was a mere lad of eighteen he began a decade-long series of intense visionary experiences that revealed to him that he is not only the Sum Totality of All Rutabagas, he is also the messenger of God-Biscuit to the peoples of planet Earth.

As noted in his hagiographic autobiodyssey, *Twitch Twice for Tiffin*, in 1937 young Gus Rasputin Nishnabotna Sni-A-Bar Freak began conducting the controversial experiments in frog-flavored yogurt for which he is world-renowned. These important experiments aroused the wrath of the **Unified Theoconservative Anti-Frog-Flavored Yogurt Alliance**[97], and while fleeing these agents of intolerance[98] he stumbled upon a hidden vault containing the original codices and palimpsests of **The Nuclear Platypus Biscuit Bible**, thought lost for millennia untold.

Disguised as a Bulgarian boat-person, Gus Rasputin Nishnabotna Sni-A-Bar Freak smuggled the book into the USA and began translating the arcane Lithuanian hieroglyphs into English. While pursuing this endeavor he was contacted by underground members of the Church of Arglebargle and, rejecting a lucrative career in theoretical dentistry, joined the Church forthwith. He made the *Honor Roll* three years in a row by selling the most cookies door-to-door of anyone in his congregation, and in only a few years had advanced through the ranks from a novice *Li'l Dumplin'* to 10th Degree *BisQuik* all the way up to 33rd Degree *Ascended Doughist Master*.

---

[97] The Unified Theoconservative Anti-Frog-Flavored Yogurt Alliance is a schismatic sect of the League in Support of Clam Enemas, having branched off in 1457 after a theological dispute over whether the plural form of 'Enema' should in fact be *Enemæ* rather than *Enemas*.

[98] Agents of *lactose intolerance*, that is.

The official Church phrenologist quickly discovered that Gus Rasputin Nishnabotna Sni-A-Bar Freak is a direct lineal descendant of not only Flavius Romulus Augustus and the Merovingian Kings, but also of the last Arglebargle Pope, the voluminous Pope Spittle the XXXL, who had been lost at sea during an inner tube race in 321 A.D. [see *The Gospel of Quzzzxzzz*, verse 48, for additional info].

Michelangelo's portrait of Pope Gus Rasputin Nishnabotna Sni-A-Bar Freak the First, titled *Portrait of the Pope As A Papal Vibration*.

With this discovery Gus Rasputin Nishnabotna Sni-A-Bar Freak became Pope Gus Rasputin Nishnabotna Sni-A-Bar Freak the First, the first Biscuitist Pope in over 1,600 years. The *Supreme Avatar of Old Skool Biscuitism*, Pope Gus is a charismatic leader, fair and just, yet able to do that which is best for the perpetuation of the Doughist Doctrine. To switch food groups for a moment, one might say that in a world populated by mere tater tots, Pope Gus is a *Tater Titan.*[99]

In 1988 Pope Gus decided to revive the Church of Arglebargle overtly, an event that rocked the corridors of global power and caused the collapse of the atheistic/anti-Biscuitist Soviet bloc countries only three years later. The Church of Arglebargle is now acknowledged as the most powerful organization in the history of humanity, a Biscuitist behemoth and Doughist juggernaut crushing all opposition in its path, leaving an indelible mark on the human species.

Recruits to the recrudescent Church were slow at first. In late 2003, however, it was rumored that Pope Gus had contracted a fatal case of the Dewey Decimal System; the proletarian masses were shocked out of complacency and realized just how empty and pointless the world would be without Pope Gus Rasputin Nishnabotna Sni-A-Bar Freak the First at the helm. As of this writing the BiscuiTemple now processes approximately 19,800 new members every second.

Besides being the Arglebargle Pope, he is also the SubGenius Pope of the Carina Galaxy; apparently a verb; a Discordian; and an ordained minister of the Universal Life Church. His friends and enemies grudgingly admire the fact that his legs are the precise length necessary to reach from his pelvis to the ground, and always are except when they're not.

[99] For example, Pope Gus is so cool that his phone's ringtone is no mere pop song snippet; each ring is the complete 15-hour opera cycle of Wagner's *The Ring of the Nibelungen.*

BIBLIOGRAPHY

The NUCLEAR PLATYPUS CHURCH OF ARGLEBARGLE
THE ONLY CULT THAT MATTERS

Research for this Holy Book was aided by perusal of the following texts:

Biscuits of Reality
by Jason Hoelscher
'zine, two issues, April-May 1986 and January-February 1987, 24 pgs.

The Nuclear Platypus Biscuit Bible
by Pope Gus Rasputin Nishnabotna Sni-A-Bar Freak the First
First edition, 1989, 36 pgs.; Second edition, 1990, 48 pgs.

The Encyclopedia Psychedelica: The Nuclear Platypus Guide to Almost Everything Relevant
Edited by Pope Gus Rasputin Nishnabotna Sni-A-Bar Freak the First
1989, 32 pgs.

The Tao of Biscuitism
by Pope Gus Rasputin Nishnabotna Sni-A-Bar Freak the First
1989, 122 pgs.

Arglebargle Indoctrination Tape #1: Praise the Glory of the God-Biscuit
by Pope Gus Rasputin Nishnabotna Sni-A-Bar Freak the First
1990, 90-minute cassette + 24 page book

The Dough Te Ching
by Ped Xing, 4182 B.C., 72 pgs.

The Iliad of Ped Xing: The Pop-Up Edition
by Ped Xing, 4163 B.C., 82,615 pgs.

Are You There God? It's Me, Aeschylus
by Robert F. Kennedy and Judy Blume, 1967, 441 pgs.

We Hold This Dough to be Self-Baking: Deistic Biscuitism and Its Role In the Affairs of Human Civilization
Edited by Tom Paine and the Keebler Elves, 1790, 111 pgs.

Trilateral Biscuitist Global-Management Techniques
by Rev. Iasonus Hoelscherus, 1973, 368 pgs.

... So He Caught the Sausage With His Pants: Adventures in Penal Code Enforcement
by Arnold Ziffel, Foreword by Prince Charles, 1972, 4 pgs.

Remembrance of Quings Past
by Marcel Proust and Leonard Shelby, 1922, 24,006 pgs.

Tractatus Biscuito-Philosophicus: Quick Recipes for Logical Positivists & Other Empiricists
by Ludwig Wittgenstein and Paula Deen, 1950, 81 pgs.

Würlde Withoute Scabs
by Rev. Speemophilocles the Aborborygmatous, 3185 B.C., 749 pgs.

The Wrath of Grapes: *Who Are You Calling Roughage?!*: **A Guide to the Resentful Worldview and Hate-Filled Subjective Interiority of Fruits & Vegetables**
by John Steinbeck and Peter Tompkins, 1970, 221 pgs.

Confessions of a Mute Palace Castrato and His Voice-Activated Prune
by Alessandro Moreschi and Helen Keller, 1921, 350 pgs.

This Book's Title: The Book With This Subtitle
by The Author of This Book, 2112, 121 pgs.

The Dismal Feast: A Festive Tale of Reciprocal Social Alienation
by Anonymous, Sr. and Anonymous, Jr., 1984, 0 pgs.

Beans and Nothingness: Toward a Phenomenological Ontology of Lentils
by Jean-Paul Sartre, Pythagoras, and Pliny the Elder, 1943, 740 pgs.

<u>Doughja-vu:</u> The face of the Biscuitist pilgrim prior
to birth and again after death, shown here as the soul
leaves the body and enters the Hereafter. There the
Biscuitist Messiah will give it a quick spritz of *Sin-B-Gon*
and send it along to be baked into its next incarnation in
The Great White Light of the Oven on High

ACKNOWLEDGMENTS

Dedicated with love to Carolyn & Rich, those who begat me.

Special thanks to: Sonya, for joining me to go fishing in the dark, and Carina Rae, Flour Power personified; Gian, Suzi, Marcel and Jackson; the Mighty Pope RevRalph Rutabaga-Simpleton the Second; St. Kory Huckleberri-Nut Vern the Last, Ph.D.; Pope (Brendan)² Darth; Doktor Philo U. Drummond Ø1; Rev. Frumerious Pre-Spiff; Rev. Sunflower-Biscuit; Soror Mollyeyllom; Frater Subma Kukabaka; Rev. Zum Splurb; Rev. Jeremzekial the Impassioned and Mother Elsie the Preserver; Rev. Amun-Ka Angular; Revs. Rob and Mark SkinGraft; Rev. Finder Fooley Borp-Poob; Rev. Ol' Sam the Unravelling Man; Project Sigma; the Indefatigable Fjor; Messrs. Ehrenworth, McGinty & Hoops; Greg the Croatian Pope; the Biscuit Bands *Babylon Exorcism*, *Acrylic Orgy*, *The Exit* and *Hypedelic*; Vintage Vinyl in U. City, MO; and Cool Stuff in Columbia, MO. A special tip o' the Biscuit to FallenArch-Bishop King BiscuitBoy and to the Rev. Wacky Exclamatus.

FallenArch-Bishop King BiscuitBoy and Pope Gus Rasputin Nishnabotna Sni-A-Bar Freak the First channeled the blessed face of God-Biscuit during a rather strange afternoon in either late 1989 or early 1990, with the aid of the first-ever public release of Photoshop. The artwork on pages 20, 41 and 93, and the circular Church logo on the back cover, is by FallenArch-Bishop King BiscuitBoy. The photo on page 107 is by St. Kory Huckleberri-Nut Vern the Last, Ph.D. and Pope Gus Rasputin Nishnabotna Sni-A-Bar Freak the First.

"Tis an ill wind that blows no minds."
　　　　　—Malaclypse the Younger, *Principia Discordia*

This book has been prepared as an educational primer for members of the Church of Arglebargle and other advanced mutants. Under no circumstances is it to be confused with inflatable peanut butter, nor should it be contemplated by those with inflatable peanut butter allergies.

LEGAL DISCLAIMERS

DISCLAIMER REGARDING THE ACCURACY OF
PROPHETIC DATA PROPOUNDED HEREIN

The information in this Holy Book has been prepared over a period of 428 bazillion years by, or on behalf of, reclusive prophets and various other difficult-to-classify entities possessed of dubious reliability and varying degrees of coherence or linguistic ability. The Nuclear Platypus Church of Arglebargle keeps the aforementioned entities on retainer for informational purposes only, and no warranty, expressed or implied, legal or spiritual, is made regarding the accuracy or even basic comprehensibility of any prophecies contained herein.

Like any Holy Book, *The Nuclear Platypus Biscuit Bible* is riddled with inconsistencies, implausible assertions and self-contradictory 'facts'. The reader should keep in mind that inconsistency, self-contradiction and wildly implausible assertions are standard conventions of the Holy Book genre, and any examples included herein should be considered within that context.

DISCLAIMER REGARDING LEGAL ADVICE

The Nuclear Platypus Church of Arglebargle has generously presented *The Nuclear Platypus Biscuit Bible* (hereinafter referred to as 'Holy Book') to provide the yearning masses of humankind with access to information about the infinite glories of the God-Biscuit. No legal advice is being given in regards to laws or speed limits in the afterlife, and no attorney-client and/or Pope-Church member and/or Deity of Dough-worshipper relationship has been created. While certain aspects of Biscuitism that affect the entirety of the universe may be discussed in a vernacular, and possibly even festive, manner herein, the laws of each state, galaxy and municipality vary, and each may have its own codes, procedures and/or protocols regarding anti-SpapOopGannopOlopOlist security measures. You are not to rely on any information provided herein in guaranteeing the future status of your soul in the afterlife and/or the hereafter and/or during inter-reincarnational pre-birth chaos.

DISCLAIMER OF BISCUITOID LIABILITY

Neither the Nuclear Platypus Church of Arglebargle nor any of its consultants or prophets shall be liable for any improper or incorrect use of the information described and/or contained herein, and assumes no responsibility for the use of said information by anyone anywhere ever, but especially not the sort of person who goes around thinking about cheeseplugs. In no event shall the Nuclear Platypus Church of Arglebargle or its agents or consultants be liable for any direct, indirect, incidental, genocidal, special, exemplary, or consequential damages (including, but not limited to, comb-over attrition; loss of limbs due to attempted bandicoot cuddling; droopy drawers caused by taco leg; or peanut envy) however caused and on any theory of liability, including negligence or otherwise, arising in any way out of lapses of comprehensibility resulting from HDTV pay-per-view smackdowns betwixt the ubiquitous Multiple Monkey Mound and Liberace's Meat-Seeking Moisture Monkey. The Nuclear Platypus Church of Arglebargle, as is its wont, is not responsible for the actions of itself or anything else, preferring to keep a low profile in assessing and/or accepting blame when and/or if things go horribly awry.

DISCLOSURE OF PRIVACY AND CONFIDENTIALITY RIGHTS OF THE DOUGHIST WORSHIPPER

By agreeing to be born into a universe ruled by an all-seeing and all-powerful omniscient deity like God-Biscuit, be aware that whether you consciously remember or not, during your *Pre-Birth Orientation Seminar* you signed and submitted paperwork[100] waiving all right to privacy.

This Holy Book has been created for the express purpose of providing a link between qualified individuals and Biscuitoid and/or Platypoid deities and/or incarnate cosmic

---

[100] Form DMT-49, *Pre-Birth Waiver of All Privacy Rights During Corporeal Manifestation Within Omniscience-Directed Universes*, on file at your local Aetheric Office of Preincarnational Initiatives.

intelligences eager to be worshipped by the aforementioned individuals. By reading *The Nuclear Platypus Biscuit Bible* you hereby acknowledge and understand that you are voluntarily disclosing that you are an individual willing to be confronted at any moment by a giant hermaphroditic fashion-obsessed 24-dimensional Biscuit with a mild speech impediment (since rectified), and that you are prepared and eager to genuflect on the spot at the first sign of the aforesaid Deity of Dough. You also hereby waive the right to sue afterward for discomfort from any possible radiation burns resulting from the spatiotemporal friction caused by squeezing the aforementioned 24-dimensional God-Biscuit into the measly 4-dimensional space-time in which you are currently corporeally manifest. This acknowledgment does not require you to give up any rights you may have under federal, state, polycosmic, interdimensional or cosmogalactic anti-discrimination or humanoid-rights laws.

DISCLAIMER OF BASIC ACCURACY OR COHERENCE
        The Nuclear Platypus Church of Arglebargle is a provider of spiritual content sometimes supplied by cosmic theomorphic entities and/or deities raised or decanted in ancient transgalactic empires with wildly alternate modes of ethics, sensibility and logic. Any and all opinions, advice, statements, services, offers, or other information or content expressed or made available by these beings, including but not limited to large masses of coagulated cheese, undercover SpapOopGannopOlopOlist agents, Frogs of and from various dispositions (of subclassifications including but not limited to Paradise-, BooHoo- Kermitoid-, Corpulent Bondage-, or Final-Frogs), those who attempt to flip one-sided pancakes, or others, are those of the respective author(s) and do not necessarily state or reflect those of the Nuclear Platypus Church of Arglebargle and shall not be used for theology-endorsement purposes. Reference herein to any specific cosmology neither constitutes nor construes nor implies an endorsement or recommendation by the Nuclear Platypus Church of Arglebargle, which is not responsible for anything, including but not limited to the contents of its very own Holy

Book, even including but not limited to the contents of this very sentence within this very disclaimer itself.

Though infallible, the Holy documents and graphics published as *The Nuclear Platypus Biscuit Bible* may contain technical inaccuracies and/or translation errors, and the book overall is frequently preposterous to an excessive degree of granularity and at a fractal level of detail. The Nuclear Platypus Church of Arglebargle and/or its schismatic sects may make improvements and/or changes to the blessed information and immortal words contained herein at any time. Furthermore, *The Nuclear Platypus Biscuit Bible* is subject to retranslation without prior notice, and the Church is not to be held responsible for spiritual angst and/or sectarian violence caused thereby.

<u>Shake it like unto a Polaroid picture</u>: Dancin' Biscuit, in Hir guise as the Dough Deva. This statue from 3760 B.C. was recently excavated from the ancient ruins of Mohenjo-daro, where Ped Xing loved to shop the outlet malls back in the day.

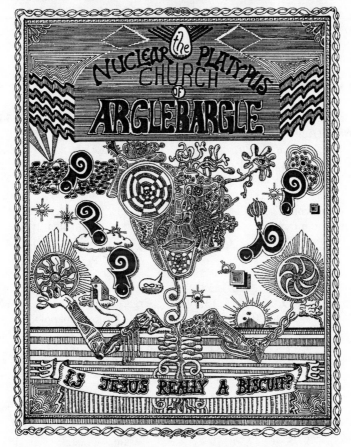

"You have to go out of your mind to use your head."
—God-Biscuit, ArglebargleOpolis Community College
Commencement address, June 11, 23.5 gazillion B.C.

INDEX

LIVE A LIFE OF SARTORIAL SPLENDOR WITH MUTANT MERCHANDISE FROM THE DEITY OF DOUGH!

Got a passion for high fashion? Visit the Divine Website (**www.god-biscuit.com**), your go-to *über*fashion headquarters! The above designs + many more are available now! Indulge yourself or the mammal of your choice with *haute couture* attire for men, women and toddlers, plus coffee mugs, stickers, baby bibs, holiday cards, hats, tote bags and more! Explore the place where Tyra, Calvin, Donatella, Jean-Paul, Ms. Wang and Messrs. Mizrahi, Givenchy and Armani find their inspiration!

WOULD THAT IT WERE AS IT IS, *SO SHALL IT BE*.

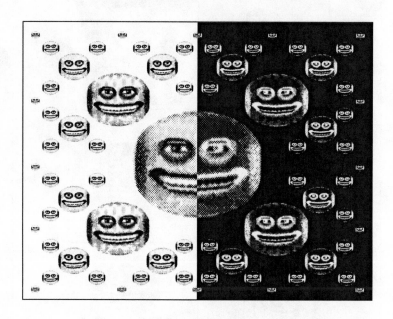

Nothing is true.

Everything is permitted.

Have a nice day.

LaVergne, TN USA
06 August 2010
192380LV00001B/170/P